NOVEL WRITING BLUEPRINT WORKBOOK

A writer's journal to help you go from idea to publication

JILL HARRIS

NB

PREFACE

Novel Writing Blueprint
a storytellers guide to the craft

Interview with the author.

What is the main message you'd like your readers to take away from this book?

You must write to the end. You must finish your book.

To do this, remember:

The story is the journey.

You set out prepared with a map, supplies, a sturdy rucksack, and an idea of what might it will be like.

But somewhere along the way, you encounter obstacles.

A landslide, an unexpected river, a bear...

You may stumble, you may fall down a crevasse. Your hand may become trapped under a heavy rock. You are trapped.

You cry out in anguish. "What can I do to make this work?"

This is how it is for all of us. Writers are weird. We love story, but making our own stories is an art.

And art, like love, is painful at times.

Which means our work is always an internal as well as an external experience.

We must step into the mind of a murderer, a warrior, a mother, a child.

We must encounter dragons, office politics, Queens, and Dukes.

We must fall in love, search for treasure, leave home, assassinate the enemy, seek revenge, suffer grief, betrayal, and injustice.

We must lose everything. We must survive that loss. Over and over again.

Whether you write genre fiction or literary works of tender existential angst, you are a storyteller. And telling stories can lead to madness. Didn't your mother warn you of this?

But nothing stops you.

You know you are a writer if you refuse to give up.

You know you can overcome every plot hole, strengthen every character arc, bring every setting alive for your reader.

All you need is practise. And a deep understanding of the craft.

You are an intrepid artist of your own inner landscape.

You will change with each story you write. You will learn the skills you need to survive from the beginning to the last page.

You bind up your wounds, kill the bear, and cross the raging river.

Some travellers have been known to hack off their own hand in order to survive.

Take a penknife. You may well have to cut scenes.

As a storyteller, your imagination is the most important item to take with you on your journey through a new book.

Nothing else matters. Nurture it. Give it space. Allow it to emerge.

Once you have mastered the craft of storytelling, when you know the terrain - and by that I mean, the purpose of each act, the beats within the acts, and the vital importance of bringing characters alive on the page - you will be able to plan less, and riff more.

Study the craft. Learn how to read the map of story.

Then, when you have finished one story, begin the next. Over time, the map will absorbed. It will be in your unconscious mind. In your blood. You will carry it everywhere you go.

It takes time. Give it time.

With patience and determination, you will develop your own novel writing blueprint.

It will guide you. Like the ancient travellers who navigated by the stars, tracked animals by their spoor, knew the winds, and the tides, and the seasons in their bones.

Never let your writing process become rigid.

There is no right or wrong way to tell a story. Listen to your readers. Give them what they need. Love, justice, survival.

Story is how we relate to the world. Stories guide us, they give life *meaning*. They make us feel. They make us think. They give us a new perspective. They entertain us, and take us away from our troubles. They nourish our souls. Story, art, music. These are the things which make us human. They are precious.

Be fearlessly curious. Be open to change. Be resilient and flexible. Bend, as the Zen masters say, with the wind.

Constantly experiment. Find new ways to tell the stories which only you can tell.

I'd like to acknowledge my students on the Open University Creative Writing course, the Frome Writers Collective, Jane Elmor, and all the writers I have taught. I have learned so much from you.

And to all the teachers who have taught me - I have so much respect for you, whether your ideas worked for me or not.

Because in the end, I found my own way. My life became story, and story became me. In essence, I found my own method of travelling.

And so will you.

Jill Harris; writer, teacher, traveller. 2017

Novel Writing Blueprint Workbook
A storytellers guide to the craft.

Jill Harris
Published by Narrative Beats

The author greatly appreciates you taking the time to read her work.
Please consider leaving a review wherever you bought the book, or telling your friends about it.

Created with Vellum

MORE BOOKS BY THE AUTHOR

Non-Fiction Books for writers:

Novel Writing Blueprint Workbook

The Write State

Other non-fiction:

The Wolf in your Bed

Fiction

Science Fiction & Fantasy writing as J. A. Harris:

Burned (Parallel World Traveller: Book 1)

Toxic (Parallel World Traveller: Book 2)

Fantasy

Tourniquet

Historical Romance with a Supernatural Twist writing as Alys Harris:

Song of the Siren

An Experiment With Flight

The Shock Box

For Jane, the most sublime writer I know.

> "Draw the art you want to see, start the business you want to run, play the music you want to hear, write the books you want to read, build the products you want to use – do the work you want to see done."
>
> —*Austin Kleon*

Are you a storyteller?

If so, you've always been one.

As children, we know who we truly are.

The pleasure of reading and writing stories often starts young.

But as the years wear away our desire to follow a creative path, we give ourselves up to the pressures of the world.

We become consumed by distraction.

In this book I'd like to help you recapture your calling.

No matter how old you are, or what work you do to make a living, you can become that which you were destined to be.

Now more than ever, we need stories to transport us, amuse us, take us on imaginary journeys which inspire us. We need to bring the killer to justice, slay the dragon, fall in love, defeat the enemy within, and transform into heroes.

The world needs more stories.

The world needs your stories.

INTRODUCTION

"Reading is the sole means by which we slip, involuntarily, often helplessly, into another's skin, another's voice, another's soul."

—*Joyce Carol Oates*

Everyone loves a good story...

Writers write to please their readers first. You create to connect.

To make a good story, you must know how to fashion one that works.

The act of writing itself is an act of self-creation which is where you, the writer, get your kicks.

For some reason, known only to your unconscious mind, making up stories and writing them down is the safest, most profound form of self development I know.

You can write a novel!

Hello and welcome to the Novel Writing Blueprint Workbook.

If you are new to writing novels you might be wondering why a novelist might need a blueprint.

Many new writers see themselves as creative artists - which they are. However - writing a novel is a craft as well as an art.

For most of us, if we sit down and just write a lot of words, we end up with, well, - a lot of words but nothing like a coherent story.

Just as a song is not the same as a feeling yet it can evoke an emotional response, a novel is not the same as a lived experience yet it can evoke the sensation of one.

And just as each artist goes through a blueprint of creation, going through a series of steps to create an album of original songs from inspirational idea into something made up of many parts including cover art, so does a writer who brings out a novel, novella or memoir into the world.

This book will help you write better stories by giving you a basic story blueprint to follow.

Enjoy the process of learning the craft. The practise of your art is important, even though it might feel trivial at times. *Because stories are what make us human.*

By following this meta-template of the entire process from idea to publication, you'll be able to write original stories in any genre. The more you write, the better your writing will be. So all you can do is to keep on writing.

More importantly, over time, your own story design process will adapt as you tweak the blueprint according to your own needs.

A craft is something that can be learned.

This is why I believe that anyone who wants to, can definitely write a novel.

When I was a child, I used to visit the pier in the seaside town where I grew up. Right at the end, was a man who made glass animals.

As I watched, he would melt coloured glass over a flame and then tease it out into the shape of a wing, or a torso, or a head. He told me once that it took many years to learn how to do it properly, and the better he got, the more he loved his work.

All creative work has a learning curve.

First, you must apprentice yourself to the craft. Just as a glass artist must learn how to work with colour, heat and composition before bringing her artistic vision to life, so a writer must learn how to shape each story he writes.

A writer must know how to catch an idea and expand on it.

She must understand the four act structure [for those who think it's 3 Acts, think again!], story beats, and how to fashion a crisis and a climax.

A writer must understand endings, twists and wrap-ups.

He needs to know when and how to utilise character arcs and plot points.

Writers also need to master the craft of completing a first draft as fast as possible. Momentum at this point is important.

There are many brilliant books on the craft of storytelling for novelists. Each of them has something useful to offer you as you work on becoming the best writer you can be.

However, you don't have to know everything in order to write your first - or even your tenth - novel or novella. In fact, many writers agree that they never stop learning the craft, which is one of things which makes this work so exciting, and pleasurable.

You can master the basics and build a body of work on that.

As you move forward, you'll adapt your writing process to reflect your experience, and each book you write will be better than the last.

Above all, unless you want to do a lot of editing, you must know how to outline and design a story that works.

Even if you've already written a few books 'by the seat of your pants', that is, without an outline, you'll certainly benefit from knowing the core beats of story blueprinting.

Most 'pantsers' have to backward engineer their work. By that I mean, once they've got down the first draft, they have to go back and test the story beats.

'Pantser' or plotter? It doesn't matter how you tell a story.

Your approach to the craft, the way you develop as a writer, is your journey, and yours alone.

What is a blueprint, anyway?

According to the Oxford dictionary, a blueprint is '. . . something which acts as a plan, model or template for others'.

This does not downgrade the importance of art when it comes to storytelling. The art of novelising is your voice. For those of you worried that using a blueprint might dampen your creative spirit, put that thought away.

A blueprint is just a framework. You get to decorate it however you like.

The writer's art is in his use of language, the kind of themes that emerge, the sort of characters he comes up with and how he imagines the flow of a story through each act.

For a novelist, a **blueprint** is a design or pattern, a template that can be applied, as we take it from the general to the particular.

Above all, a novel writing blueprint gives you the overarching pattern of the creation of any story in any genre. This is the craft of storytelling.

What is the future for authors?

Advanced forms of AI are 'learning' how to write novels. Remember, computer software is all about templates and patterns.

However, you—as a bone fide human being—still have something to offer as a writer of stories: **your voice.**

The way you use words is unique to you. Your worldview, life experiences, family, social, geographical, and cultural background, hopes, fears, desires and disappointments are also pretty unique. These things will be woven into the fabric of every novel you write.

And that's a good thing.

It's what will make your work stand out.

Even if computers get really, really good at making generic stories, they'll never have the visceral knowledge of language and human thought.

They cannot know what it is to live within the skin of a living body. They will never have stifled their cries as they were beaten as a child, or laughed at the sight of a huge wave crashing on the beach.

They will never have made love, lost someone they love or driven too fast down a highway late at night with the moon chasing them.

In fact, as so many independently published authors are saying, there's never been a better time to be an author.

You can write your book in six months or less, edit it, outsource a proofreader, get a great cover design, publish it yourself for worldwide distribution (as an ebook, print book and audio book) and earn greater royalties than traditional publishers will ever pay you.

On top of that, the global market of readers is growing, and readers are hungry for good stories, well told.

With a novel writing blueprint, you can develop your own writing process that will help you write the best books you can for an audience of readers who love to read.

So, the point of a novel writing template/blueprint, for human beings, is to set the writer free. So, don't worry about AI and computerised authors taking over the world! Our work, creative work, is best done by other living humans because our organic, living minds are set up for story. In other words, we actually understand the world around us best through story.

But what is a story?

In essence, a story is an interesting journey.

An interesting journey is always about *relationships*. And *trouble*.

As a writer, you think about both the internal and external relationships of your Main Character (MC from here on), and the trouble that comes from your MC trying to achieve a difficult goal.

A story also has an embedded code within it.

Some people call this code *story structure,* story beats, the Hero's Journey or the three/four acts of a story.

We all understand how it feels to enjoy a well-designed story. Yet this doesn't mean we know how to apply it. In the same way that we all understand how to use a table, but that doesn't mean we know how to make one.

This is why so many writers start a novel, get to around 30,000 words of a a novel, and then fizzle out. If this has happened to you, be reassured, it's a very common experience.

Although you know you should have a beginning, middle and an end, the question is how do you design such things? How do you create rising action? How do you craft an ending that truly satisfies?

When I started out writing novels, the big issue I kept having was this:

I've read so many books and watched hundreds of films, so I know *what* a story looks like. It has a beginning, a middle bit and an ending. It isn't the *what* I need to know. It's the *how*.

A novel writing blueprint is the *how*.

If you know how to truly shape a story, you can create an original piece of fiction that moves from an opening scene to the 'all is lost' moment. By understanding design and applying a series of structural or narrative 'beats', a blueprint will allow you to outline and, therefore, write, any story in any genre—from your inciting incident to the wrap-up scene at the end.

To be human is to learn through stories, to think in stories, to be entertained through stories, to live stories and to tell stories.

So, let's get working on your novel.

But first, you must make sure you've put time aside that is free from distraction.

It isn't easy to carve out creative time. Whether you're working full time and have a family and are juggling multiple commitments, time is a finite resource.

If you're very lucky, you'll have someone bring you food and drink, wash your clothes, mop your artistic brow, and tidy your house while you bash away on your keyboard. Most people, though, find a way to write in the midst of a hectic life.

And you will too. Somehow.

An hour a day is a good slice of time, although don't worry if you have to squeeze a longer period of time into a weekend.

Whether you're a daily writer or a binge writer, make sure you carry a notebook around with you to jot down random ideas, scene settings or character sketches.

Time for thinking is just as important as the writing itself. I guarantee that the deeper you go into the world of novel writing, the more you'll want to carve out time to do it. Look on it as a positive addiction.

Meanwhile, when it's time to work on your novel, do these things:

- Turn off your phone and shut down the Internet.
- Put a 'Do Not Disturb Me Please' sign on your door.
- Make sure you have access to the refreshments of your choice.
- You are about to enter your writing cave, so make it as comfortable as possible.

Part One

PREWRITING PROCESS

Chapter One

NOTEBOOKS

"It's not wise to violate the rules until you know how to observe them."

— *T. S. Elliot.*

NOTEBOOKS

There are rules to telling a good story

There is a joke about the rules of storytelling. There are three of them. But nobody knows what they are.

The truth, a story does need certain elements. Here are a few of them, in no particular order:

- Beats and turns.
- Story arcs.
- Character development.
- Conflict.
- Obstacles.
- Inner and outer goals.
- Thresholds.
- Sacrifice.

- Try-fail cycles...

Once you know them, you can do what you like. You can even pretend there are no rules.

When there are no rules - the natural storyteller

Many writers absorb their own 'novel writing blueprint', and it means they can write much faster.

Some even develop an unconscious story outline, meaning they can tell stories which work beautifully without much pre-planning.

In other words, they have become a natural storyteller.

My hope is that this book will help you to do just that!

The Novel Writing Process

Before we begin the process of writing your novel, I'd like you to get hold of TWO notebooks and a selection of pens.

Notebook 1: Your Rough Book

Notebook 1 is for stray thoughts, story ideas, creative writing exercises and anything else that inspires you or hooks your attention.

It could be a quote, a snippet of conversation, graffiti, character sketches, descriptions of settings and so on.

When you're out and about, you might prefer to make notes on your phone or computer.

Get into the habit of taking notes wherever you are. Think of your rough book as your artist's sketchbook, an essential item in your writer's toolkit.

Keep it in with you at all times. Create a new habit. Write one sentence in it every day.

Notebook 2: Your Writer's Journal

Most writers keep a separate notebook as a journal. This second notebook is a record of your internal journey as you develop the craft.

It's also a good place to write personal thoughts, events and secrets. Keep it by your bed.

If you like, there is a workbook companion to the *Novel Writing Blueprint* that is full of prompts to get your novel written.

You might prefer to make notes on your phone or computer. If you can though, use a paper notebook. It's always a good thing for a writer. Many people think the act of writing with a pen on paper has a certain quality to it, as if it gives you a deeper access to the unconscious mind where your imagination lurks.

When I'm out and about, I often write short sentences in the 'Notes' app on my phone.

Anything that resonates strongly with me goes here. Here's an example of one of them: *An island on the horizon always draws you to it* . . . .

I don't know when, if or how I will use this, but I really like the image it conjures up of an island that seems to call to someone.

It also makes me think about the human quality of yearning for adventure, something I relate to and will definitely give to one of my characters in the next book I write.

Phone apps are great for catching ideas on the run, but I urge you to use a book made of paper too. Carry it around with you as often as you can. Find a size and shape you like.

Think of your notebook as your artist's sketchbook. It's a playground of ideas and inspirations. You don't have to just use words either. I am a big fan of mind maps. Sometimes I draw things out as well. This is a way of 'netting the butterflies' or catching creative thoughts as they float through my mind.

You might think you'll remember your ideas, and some of them you will. But most of them you won't. So get into the habit of taking notes.

An artist is a journalist of the seen and the unseen world we live in.

WRITE ABOUT A JOURNALIST REPORTING ON SOMETHING IN THE UNSEEN WORLD...

Remember, the most important thing about a notebook, sketch

pad, notes app or whatever is that you regularly read what you've written.

This is the primordial mud of your creative process.

Dredge through the pages, and you'll find diamonds in the slime.

OWL: Whatever kind of artist you are, the psychology of creative production remains the same.

Every painter, songwriter, sculptor, photographer, poet or choreographer will go through these stages in order to produce a new, and original piece of work:

◦Preparation: Analyse the work of other, similar artists.

◦Incubation: Unconsciously sift through the work of others.

◦Insight: Bam! A new idea occurs.

◦Evaluation: Decide whether the idea is worth working on.

◦Elaboration: Do the work. This is the longest phase.

To write a novel, this can be boiled into three main stages:
OUTINING
WRITING
LEARNING

PREPARATION FOR AN AUTHOR MEANS READING THE WORK OF OTHERS. WHAT ARE YOU READING RIGHT NOW? WHY DO LIKE THIS STORY? WHAT IS THE MAIN CHARACTER LIKE? WHAT IS THE VILLAIN/ANTAGONIST LIKE?

THE STAGES OF FICTION WRITING

In 1978, Malcolm Cowley wrote about the stages of creating a work of fiction:

There would seem to be four stages in the composition of a story.

First comes the germ of the story, then a period of more or less conscious meditation.

Then the first draft.

Finally the revision, which may be simply 'pencil work' as John O'Hara calls it. That is, you make minor changes in wording—or perhaps you end up writing several drafts based on your original story, and end up writing what amounts to a new work.

If you compare the two different models of creativity, you can see that most writers can only truly evaluate their work when it's done.

Therefore the 'evaluation' stage of creativity comes after the 'elaboration' or writing first draft stage.

Over the years, I've broken down the craft of making a novel into a model I call *OWL*. It has three main stages.

These stages incorporate all of the above and condense them into a model you can use as your novel writing blueprint:

HAVE YOU GOT A STORY GERM/IDEA/SPARK IN MIND RIGHT NOW? IF SO, WRITE IT DOWN, EVEN IF IT'S JUST A TITLE.

OWL = OUTLINING, WRITING, LEARNING

1. **Outlining**:

This includes what Cowley calls the story 'germ'. The process might include all or some of these:

◦ Prewriting: Analysing and absorbing other stories. Taking notes and focusing on creative writing exercises.

◦ Research: Finding out as much as you need to know to begin writing your novel.

◦ Organising/Planning: Making a working outline so you can test the story structure for plot holes. Now you have the broad strokes of each scene.

By the end of this stage, you'll have lots of notes and a working outline of your novel.

So, outlining is many things. It is preparation, incubation, planning, and insight combined.

You read other writers, analyse the story structure of books, films, plays, radio and TV dramas.

Your unconscious mind makes connections and feeds them back to you in unusual ways, through dreams or sudden moments of aha!

You then use your knowledge of story structure to prepare a written outline of your story.

2. **Writing**:

This is your first draft. It should be done fast. The key to writing fast (for most writers) is to freewrite from an outline.

It should be a breathless romp from beginning to end. Dorothy Canfield Fisher described this phase as being similar to skiing down a steep hill, uncertain as to whether she had the smarts to get down in one piece.

◦ Writing first draft: *Write fast.*

◦ Freewriting: Freewriting from a structured outline. But you don't have to use an outline. If you like to discover the story during this phase, that's fine. Accept the feeling of being out of control!

3. **Learning**: This is in everything you do.

It is your everyday experience of life as well as writing. A creative person is constantly absorbing the world around her. This is the grounding of art.

As Cowley points out, learning and improving, can lead to a total reworking of the entire story. This is something I had to do with my first two novels.

In many ways, learning from the last story you wrote, is the stage where you learn the most.

That's because during revision, you're looking at both the art (writing style, language use, metaphor etc.) and the craft, and evaluating both of them.

Sometimes you have to scrap thousands of words and start again.

The things you learn at this phase then feed back into a new outlining phase.

I like to call this stage the 'learning loop' because of the way it connects with and improves your writing overall.

Many people think of this phase as just the editing phase, but it's so much more. It can include all of these:

◦Self-editing

◦Outsourcing to a professional editor

◦Making changes, cutting out sections, rewriting a few scenes or adding new ones in

◦Rewriting the whole thing

Everything you do during this stage of your novel writing blueprint is an opportunity for learning your craft.

HAVE YOU BEEN THROUGH A COMPLETE OWL CYCLE YET? IF SO, WHAT WORKED? HOW DID YOU COPE WITH GETTING STUCK? WHAT INSPIRED YOU? WHERE COULD YOU IMPROVE YOUR PROCESS?

THE FUNNEL OF AMAZING IDEAS.

Sit down, close your eyes and take a couple of deep breaths.

Imagine there is a giant funnel attached to the top of your head.

It is wider at the top so it can receive plenty of story ideas directly from your surroundings.

The ancient Greeks believed songs, stories, poems, pictures etc. exist in the external environment and all the artist has to do is become aware of it.

For the purposes of this exercise, imagine this to be true. There they are, all the brilliant story concepts, themes, characters and plots floating down into the funnel attached to your brain.

As the funnel gets closer to your head, it is much narrower. This is because it is filtering out anything which might not work for you. Only the best ideas are allowed to enter your mind and lodge there until you need them.

Keep imagining this for five or ten minutes. You might like to visualise story ideas as gorgeous, intricate little machines.

You don't need to know what these ideas are specifically, just that they are great, and they are *yours*.

When you've finished, make a cup of your favourite hot beverage and open up your notebook. A story is ready to be born.

WHAT IDEAS CAME TO YOU AFTER YOU VISUALISED THE FUNNEL OF AMAZING IDEAS?

Chapter Two

IDEAS, RESEARCH & GLORIOUS ACCIDENTS

"You don't get lucky without preparation, and there's no sense in being prepared if you're not open to the possibility of a glorious accident."

—*Twyla Tharp*

WHAT ARE YOU CURIOUS ABOUT? WRITE DOWN THE FIRST THING THAT COMES INTO YOUR MIND.

EVERYTHING IN THE CREATIVE PROCESS IS FLEXIBLE

Try out all the suggestions in this book.

Some will work for you and some will not. Adapt each method to suit you.

This is how you attain mastery over your own artistry!

What is prewriting?

Prewriting is everything you do before you sit down to write your first draft.

When you decide to write a novel, it's tempting to begin by going straight to the page and banging away on the keyboard.

However, for most of us, this does not work. Especially if you're just starting out.

Most people do not set out on a journey without a destination, and some idea of the route.

Prewriting or preparing to write your book is always time well spent.

It gives you a chance to check your ideas.

The organised author knows the genre, characters, setting and plot before she begins to write.

Remember, by designing your book first, you'll save time later when it comes to editing. Also, you'll be working with the natural creative process of your mind, which means exploring an idea first.

To make something new, you should have at least a rough sketch of what it's going to be before you devote time, resources and energy creating it.

To help you develop your own novel writing process, I suggest you include in the prewriting stage:

- research,
- genre decisions,
- character sketches,
- settings,
- and a plot outline.

HOW LONG DO SHOULD YOU SPEND PREWRITING?

This is entirely up to you.

At first, it may take three months of preparation before you begin to write.

If you write long, historical novels, or epic fantasies set in worlds you've created beforehand, it might always take this long or even longer.

However, most authors speed up over time.

If you write a few novels in a series, you'll do most of the work on the first novel, and be able to start writing the rest of them fairly quickly.

If you want to get a finished novel done in three months—which is entirely possible—then you'll probably only spend around two weeks on this part of your writing process.

If you want to write a novel in a month, then four or five days of prewriting is about right.

HOW LONG DO YOU WANT TO SPEND PREWRITING YOUR NEXT NOVEL? WHEN CAN YOU FIND THE TIME? WHAT KIND OF RESEARCH DO YOU NEED TO DO? COULD YOU DO SOME OF IT AS YOU WRITE? MAKE NOTES.

In summary, prewriting is essentially everything you do before you write a single word.

The two kinds of prewriting are:

Conscious, and unconscious.

Conscious Prewriting

This is when you use cognitive processes to make decisions.

Much of this book will give you an overview on how to approach this aspect.

In conscious prewriting, you turn the full beam of your creative attention on deliberately.

Research

What do you need to know before you start? Gather images, maps, information about weapons, methods of flight or whatever you think will help.

Historical writing takes a little more time. Do as much as you need to before you write, but no more.

Some writers leave spaces in their first draft with notes to remind them of further research. You might want to use this method. If there's something you need to know, but don't want to stop to find it yet, just do this [NAME of battle outside Moscow & date...]. Then write on.

Others like to dart online and pick up the relevant information as fast as possible.

Find out what works for you.

There is no right or wrong way of doing this.

More on research later.

AS A STORYTELLER, YOU NEED TO BECOME ALIVE AND AWAKE TO YOUR OWN FASCINATIONS.

Here are 10 random nouns that came into my mind at this moment:

Lantern
Sword

Hotel
Guitar
Dog
Rain
Flower
Ship
Eyes
Child

WRITE DOWN 10 CONCRETE NOUNS OF YOUR OWN.

Next, think about abstract nouns. Here are ten I just thought of:

Justice
Love
Power
Science
Belief
Grief
Awe
Fear
Anger
Desire

WRITE DOWN 10 ABSTRACT NOUNS. WRITE QUICKLY, DON'T THINK TOO HARD ABOUT THIS EXERCISE.

NOW LINK EACH CONCRETE NOUN TO ONE OF YOUR ABSTRACT ONES. YOU'LL COME UP WITH SOME INTERESTING COMBINATIONS, SUCH AS:

The Ship of Justice
The Power of a Flower
The Dog of Anger
The Guitar of Desire
The Sword of Grief

Let your mind play around with these ideas. Doodle, noodle, and sketch.

Don't think, just play. It's important. You're a wordsmith, go bend those ideas with the flame of your unconscious mind.

Imagnineer like you just don't care!

Waste nothing.

Make these short creative writing exercises work hard. They are all part of writing your novel.

For example, from this small list, I know I'll include all the concrete nouns in my next novel. I had no idea there would be a dog with a link to anger in it, but I'll make him an important aspect of the plot.

When it comes to abstract concepts, the words you've just written have told you exactly what kind of themes appeal to you.

Work with them, and watch as they emerge in your novels.

Of course, with conscious prewriting you can go as far as you like.

Draw maps.

Describe a person in a couple of sentences.

Make up names.

Write summaries of story ideas.

The purpose of gathering ideas for your novel may look odd to those around you.

They may think you're staring into space, havn't had a good night's sleep, or are suffering from a hangover.

Yet all writers write in their heads as well as on paper, computer, voice recorder and phone apps.

We write while we're shopping, driving, walking and even when we're at a social gathering.

The more novels you write, the more time you will spend in this frame of mind.

As soon as your mind snags on something, take notes!

Outlining a novel starts with an idea. Ideas come from capturing your fascinations.

Question = Where do ideas come from?

Answer = Everywhere. It's your worldview, the things which appeal to you that give life to your stories.

Which is good news, I'm sure you'll agree.

ALWAYS BE OPEN TO GLORIOUS ACCIDENTS. HERE'S A LIST OF PROMPTS TO WRITE ABOUT IN YOUR NOTEBOOK IF YOU GET STUCK IN A SNOWSTORM OR SIMILAR:

- Getting snowed in with a stranger.
- A character who is good yet has flaws and is someone who inspires you.
- A difficult, criminal or antagonistic person who nevertheless fascinates you.
- An opening scene.
- A woman who loses her faith.
- Star-crossed lovers.
- A theme you want to explore.
- A setting you're drawn to.
- An old story (Bible story, myth, legend, fairy story, fable) you want to tell in a new way.
- A dream or a daydream.
- A story on the news.
- A family relationship dynamic you'd like to explore, such as siblings, mother/daughter, father/son and so on.
- An event, such as the destruction of the Twin Towers in New York, that you're obsessed with.
- The Holy Grail with vampires . . . or some other odd combination of myths and legends.
- A small town full of strange happenings.

PICK ONE NOW. SET A TIMER FOR 8 MINUTES. JUST WRITE.

NOW PICK ANOTHER ONE. WORK IN ONE OF YOUR CONCRETE + ABSTRACT NOUN IDEAS:

Read back over what you just wrote. Any surprises? Unexpected ideas are the writer's treasure.

SET A TIMER FOR ANOTHER 8 MINUTES, AND EXPAND YOUR INITIAL NOTES INTO A SCENE. INCLUDE ALL THE SENSES. WHAT DOES YOUR VIEWPOINT CHARACTER THINK ABOUT WHAT SHE IS EXPERIENCING? WHAT IS THE SETTING LIKE? SOUNDS? SMELLS? TASTES?

UNCONSCIOUS PREWRITING

Spontaneous eruption of creativity are to be encouraged!

You are always prewriting.

In your sleeping, and waking dreams.

Daydreaming is essential to the creative mind. It occurs whenever you're drawn to a particular person, place, object or event or when you find yourself staring at a sunset, brick wall or a woman stooping to pick up her child.

Write down your dreams in your journal. They are powerful story starters.

Although you're technically conscious when you're daydreaming, it's still a dreamlike state.

Creative people daydream a lot. You might have got into trouble for it as a child. I certainly did!

Often, when we come out of such a state, we quickly forget whatever it was we were thinking about. As a writer, you need to train yourself to *take notes*. Before that crazy idea drifts away.

This kind of thinking, or imagineering as I like to call it, is usually lost.

Yet the more you take notice of these flights of fancy, the more useful they become to your writing process.

PRESENT MOMENT: TAKE A BREAK AND TUNE INTO YOUR OWN THOUGHTS. WRITE DOWN A COUPLE OF SENTENCES ABOUT WHAT IS OCCUPYING YOUR MIND RIGHT NOW. A SONG LYRIC? A RECENT BREAK-UP? THE POLITICAL CLIMATE? THE COLOUR OF RAIN? THE HOMELESS PERSON WHO SLEEPS IN THE SAME DOORWAY EVERY NIGHT? A TRAIN WRECK YOU SAW ON THE NEWS?

Now, let's think about the dreams we have in our sleep.

Whenever the emotional content of a dream is still with you when you wake, all you have to do it take notice. To take notice, it's essential to *take notes!*

Memory of a Dream.

WRITE DOWN THE MOST INTENSE DREAM/NIGHTMARE YOU'VE EVER HAD.

Write it in first person, present tense, for example: I am on the beach when I see the tidal wave coming towards me. It is moving so fast I know I'm going to die ...

Be sure to include the emotional content of the dream, for example: I'm so frightened I cannot move, cannot take my eyes off the huge, dark wall of roiling water ...

When you've finished writing the dream, think about how this might become a scene in a novel.

If you're writing a romance, perhaps two people meet in the aftermath of a tsunami [or whatever your dream content involved].

If you want to write a thriller, maybe the tidal wave has been set off by an underground nuclear explosion that your hero failed to prevent.

If you're interested in writing a fantasy, perhaps the tidal wave wrecks a ship carrying the dragon of power.

WRITE DOWN HOW THIS DREAM COULD BECOME A SCENE IN YOUR NOVEL.

Chapter Three

GENRE AWAREENESS & ORGANISATION

"Writing is writing, and stories are stories. Perhaps the only true genres are fiction and non-fiction. And even there, who can be sure?"
—*Tanith Lee.*

GENRE AWARENESS IS THE KEY TO WRITING A NOVEL THAT SELLS

Know your genres. Know their tropes. Ingest them and soon, you'll be able to start a story knowing it will please readers.

Because this is the true work of telling stories:

Making readers happy they read your book.

And most of them want to know what to expect from a story. If you examine literary fiction, most of it fits a distinct genre.

Wuthering Heights? Romance with a hint of the paranormal.

1984? Dystopian.

Lord of the Rings? Epic fantasy.

James Bond? Spy Thriller.

Organisation is the Key to Creativity

I'll repeat that. *Organisation is the key to creativity.* Who'd have thought it?

But surely, I hear you cry, *writing a novel is a creative thing, and I should be able to just sit down and let it pour out of me like water from a magic tap.*

Well, yes, some authors can do that. Stephen King famously does no outlining/organising at all. He sits down and the magic tap turns on.

It occurs to me that he probably has an innate story structure compass, an internal novel writing blueprint that he works from, and therefore doesn't understand how most of us can get very lost if we try to write by the seat of our pants.

However, most of us are not the King. But that doesn't mean we can't be productive novelists.

All you need is a great writing process, which, over time, will become internalised.

The main things you need to organise, at least in your own mind, before you start outlining and writing your novel are listed here:

- Genre: What type of story is it?
- Story people: Who is your story about?
- Setting: Where does it all happen?
- Premise: What is the main hook or story question?

Genre Awareness

Genre awareness is the key to writing a novel that sells.

Yes, you have to pick one for now, although you don't have to write in the same one forever.

I don't intend to. I've started with a science fiction and fantasy trilogy, but I also write romance, epic fantasy and will work on some crime thrillers too over the next few years.

Of course, you can mash up any two or three genres as long as you know what you're doing.

WHAT GENRES DO YOU ENJOY READING[INCLUDE LITERARY FICTION AS A GENRE]?

And for those of you who are keen to write a literary novel, *literary fiction is also a genre*, as is 'women's fiction' and 'contemporary fiction', although these last two seem far too vague to be useful to the would-be novelist.

You can be writing about a woman who likes to go shopping a lot and that's 'women's fiction' apparently.

But what if she gets involved in a murder? Then it becomes crime.

What if she falls in love with a soldier? Romance.

What if she stalks a famous film star in her spare time? Psychological thriller.

What if she suffers existential angst over her lack of self-fulfilment whilst shopping? Literary fiction.

Anyway, now you can see that genre is not only useful, it's also your friend because this is how your readers find you. Not only that, genre guides you when you create your outline.

Originally, genre was a way for booksellers and publishers to categorise their authors' books.

For many authors writing today, there is a clear path from deciding to write a novel to self-publishing it and making it available on Amazon, Kobo, iBooks, and so on.

The royalties are much higher if you do this, so you don't need to sell as many books to make a living from your writing.

For those of us who do self-publish, it's important that our readers can find our work. Genre placing makes this much easier for readers to find you.

Genre also helps you understand the tone and texture of your story.

A romance must have a happy ever after (the HEA) ending.

Thriller readers want a fast pace. They want to see the MC or Hero of the book win against an threatening enemy.

Mystery readers like to see the crime solved.

Science fiction novels should include a bit of science. Fantasy novels usually have a bit of magic and, often, dragons.

You have loads of genres and sub-genres to choose from, and you can do a mixture if you like.

The best place to explore genre is on Amazon. Have a look at the genre categories listed under your favourite novels.

If you decide to self-publish your story, this is one place where you'll make your book available. Every book is categorised according to genre at the bottom of the book description on the sales page. Write down the genre category of the last five novels you read. This will give you a strong indication that you might enjoy writing in the same genre.

I particularly enjoy looking at the genres defined on the Goodreads website (www.goodreads.com).

I was astounded to discover 'Sinister Literature' and 'Historical Ghost Fiction' here, and I will probably read some of that before the year is out.

GO TO GOODREADS AND MAKE A LIST OF GENRES YOU'VE NEVER HEARD OF BEFORE. YOU CAN EVEN MAKE UP A FEW OF YOUR OWN!

Tropes

Every genre has its common tropes or literary motifs. TV Tropes (www.tvtropes.org) is a great website for exploring tropes.

Some of them are cliches, but some of them fall into the category of *reader expectations*.

Remember, if you want to publish you are writing for your reader. That means you make a promise to that reader. And you won't let them down.

Make sure you know the difference between cliches and expectations in your chosen genre.

MAKE A LIST OF TROPES FOR ONE OF THE NEW GENRES YOU'VE DISCOVERED ON GOODREADS.

IF YOU HAVEN'T ALREADY, WRITE A LIST OF THE LAST FIVE NOVELS YOU ENJOYED READING.

WHAT GENRE CATEGORY ARE THEY LISTED IN ON AMAZON? ON GOODREADS? WRITE DOWN THEIR GENRE NEXT TO THE TITLE ABOVE.

If you're anything like me, you probably read in many different genres. I decided to write science fiction and fantasy because I love it, but I read a lot of other stuff too.

NOW, WRITE A FEW SENTENCES ABOUT ONE OF THE GENRES YOU LIKE. WHAT DO YOU LIKE ABOUT IT? WHY?

For example, I like science fiction and fantasy because it's a great place to explore the *current* psychological and philosophical state of the human condition in a metaphorical way. I can also let my imagination go wild, which is always fun.

MAKE A DECISION NOW ABOUT WHAT GENRE YOU'LL WRITE YOUR CURRENT NOVEL IN. MAKE A LIST OF THE MOST COMMON TROPES OF YOUR CHOSEN GENRE.

WRITE ABOUT WHAT EXCITES YOU ABOUT THIS GENRE. PICK A GENRE TROPE FROM YOUR LIST, AND WRITE ABOUT HOW YOU COULD MAKE IT FRESH. WHAT TYPE OF CHARACTER MIGHT BE REALLY TESTED BY YOUR NEW VERSION OF THIS TROPE?

Chapter Four

RESEARCH

"Do research. Feed your talent. Research not only wins the war on cliche, it's the key to victory over fear and it's cousin, depression."

—Robert McKee

BEFORE AND AFTER RESEARCH

You'll find it simpler to do some research before you write your novel and some afterwards.

Do what you can at the start of your process. I guarantee you will realise there are other things you need to know while you're writing your first draft.

In that case, make a note of what it might be in brackets, such as [How far away is Mars from Earth and how long would it take to get there?], [What is the speed of light?], and then move on. If you choose to check things while writing, do it fast.

You should always be moving forward as you work on your novel.

Research is directed noodling.

Noodling: to improvise in an informal way

Noodling: to improvise in an informal way

Personally, I love researching, finding stuff out and all forms of noodling.

Set specific time aside for this. You can carve out an hour, more or less, to sit down and find out what you need to know to move forward with your novel.

Today, most of us have hectic lives. We juggle jobs, children, family commitments, exercise, housekeeping, social events, hobbies, holidays and lovers.

WRITE DOWN DAYS OF THE WEEK AND TIMES WHEN YOU CAN RESEARCH YOUR NOVEL.

SO, HOW DO YOU FIND THE TIME TO WRITE?

Simple. You take it away from something less important.

Do you need to watch TV for four hours straight?

Can you get up earlier to work on your novel?

Stay up later?

Can you sneak off in your lunch hour for some well-directed noodling?

What about the commute? Perhaps you could work on the train?

The reality is that you'll do what you're motivated to do.

If you really want to write a novel, you'll find the time. We give things up—the kind of things that bring only momentary satisfaction such as TV or mindless Internet snuffling.

Besides, research is interesting.

Many authors love this bit of the process, which makes sense because creative people are, by nature, curious magpies.

During this stage of your writing process, you'll be alternating between idea gathering, taking notes and thinking.

Remember to daydream. Thinking about your novel is as important as anything else you do right now, although it's best to make a note of your most creative thoughts, if possible.

A lot of writers talk about a daily writing/working on their novel habit.

This is a great bit of advice, but for some of us, it isn't possible.

Perhaps, for practical reasons, you're a binge writer. In this case, you might only have four hours on a weekend.

That's fine too. *There is no right or wrong way to do this*. As long as it's something you do on a regular basis and in a way that suits your lifestyle.

I started off as a binge writer, and I don't always write every day, although I do some kind of work on my novels and non-fiction books every weekday.

The muse is always with you

I think this is a good time to discuss the muse or muses.

In ancient times, it was believed that creative inspiration came from the gods.

The muses were nine ethereal beauties. They whispered poems, songs, epic lyrics and other fully formed works into the ear of the poet or musician. All a creative soul had to do was sit down and take dictation.

It seems many of us still think it's only worthwhile to write when the muse is loud and clear.

Not true.

A lot of people think that they have to be 'in the mood' for creative work. In other words, they await the inspiration of the muse.

Those who wait in this way often don't do the work.

Write this down on a sticky note and put it where you can see it:

The muse is always with me.

WRITE A DESCRIPTION OF YOUR MUSE. IS YOUR MUSE MALE OR FEMALE? DOES HE WEAR FLOATING GOWNS OR LEATHERS? DOES SHE HAVE WINGS OR RIDE A MOTOR BIKE?

Many authors find that the work they do when they feel inspired is no better than what they produce when they feel dry and tired and distinctly una*mused*.

What to Do with Your Notes

So, you have found a precious hour to sit down and work on your book.

You've shut down the Internet and let everyone know you must not be disturbed on pain of pain.

What next?

By now, you have a collection of random stuff in your notebook. You want to get on and write your book, but wait. Make sure you have everything you need for the journey.

What is emerging as you noodle?

Freud said that all creative work is a form of adult play. Cultivate this attitude as you sift through your notes.

WHAT KINDS OF SITUATIONS DO YOU LIKE TO READ ABOUT? HOW DO YOU EXPLORE THEM IN YOUR NOTES? HOW CAN YOU EXPLORE THEM FURTHER?

WHAT TYPES OF CHARACTERS FASCINATE YOU? WHY?

WHAT TYPES OF SETTINGS ARE YOU DRAWN TO? DESCRIBE THEM USING ALL FIVE SENSES.

WHAT DO YOU NEED TO KNOW? MAKE A LIST OF THINGS TO RESEARCH.

It might be that your notes are full of ideas about a certain country, political system, historical time period or specific genre.

In my novel *Toxic*, I realised pretty early on that I needed to know more about current scientific theories concerning parallel worlds.

At first, I rushed in full of enthusiasm and wrote my first draft without research or planning. What a mess it was! But I learned my lesson well. I'm still writing the science fiction and fantasy series I started back then, but with a lot more knowledge about multiple world theories and what they mean.

After a few sessions of researching your initial idea germs, you'll begin to see something emerging from your notes that grabs you and won't let you go.

Perhaps there's a character you want to write about.

It might be just a name or a title.

It could be a twist ending, a famous person, or a fascination with robberies.

Maybe you have come to something quite specific.

Perhaps you realise you'd like to write a crime thriller called *Daylight Robbery* about a character called, Harry, an old man who dreams of doing one last heist.

Maybe you don't have a title or a name, but you see that you want to write a romance novel about an artist and an assassin.

Perhaps you need to discover more about watercolour painting, guns, bank heists, jail, space travel or the stages of love (yes folks, there are certain, recognisable micro-stages we all go through when we fall in love, and all romance writers need to know them).

Perhaps you need to find out more about a certain city because it's the best setting for your work.

If you can't visit a place, go there on the Internet. This is a time to open yourself up to the joys of the Web. I have found most of my scientific research is well served by YouTube videos as well as books and blogs.

Make research notes in your notebook.

Play around with the things you discover. Keep asking yourself the question, 'what if?'

MAKE A LIST OF SOME INTERESTING 'WHAT IFS':

In my novel, *Toxic*, these questions kept popping up:

What if a scientist, stranded on a world where human evolution never happened, found a way to create humanoid companions?

What could go wrong?

RESEARCH AS MUCH AS YOU NEED TO, BUT DON'T LET IT GO ON TOO LONG.

As you write through your novel, you'll find there are many other things you need to find out. But, for now, decide how long this aspect of your process will last and then stop.

Of course, some authors need to spend more time on this than others. It took me a long time to grapple with all the multiple world theories out there.

If you're writing historical fiction, your research might go on for six months or more.

The more books you write, the more you'll come to know when to stop researching and start organising everything you have so far.

After a research session, put your new notes aside.

NOW USE THE RESEARCH YOU'VE DONE AND THESE WRITING PROMPTS FOR A QUICK SESSION OF FUN AND FREE THINKING ON THE PAGE.

1. What if? [*An elderly bank robber decided to steal the crown jewels.*]

2. What could go wrong? [*Her grandson might find out about it and insist on coming too.*]

3. What's the worst that could happen? [*A rival criminal from the old days kidnaps the grandson's girlfriend in order to get a cut of the heist.*]

4. How could I write this idea germ into any *genre* I like? Play around with all sorts of genres before you settle on one. You might find there's another angle on this 'What If' that you'd like to explore:

Crime? *[The ageing robber is murdered, and a cop has to solve the crime.]*

Romance? *[The girlfriend has to escape and help her boyfriend start a new life.]*

Fantasy? *[The bank robber is on another world with magic and dragons.]*

Thriller? *[An ex-marine suffering from PTSD finds out about the kidnapping and gets involved.]*

Science fiction? *[This all takes place on a spaceship hurtling towards Earth.]*

Literary? *[A divorced journalist covers the court case and suffers lots of existential angst over the meaning of his life whilst drinking too much coffee.]*

You get the idea. Play around with lots of different scenarios.

Chapter Five

STORY GOAL

"Have you got any soul?" a woman asks the next afternoon. That depends, I feel like saying; some days yes, some days no. A few days ago I was right out; now I've got loads, too much, more than I can handle. I wish I could spread it a bit more evenly, I want to tell her, get a better balance, but I can't seem to get it sorted. I can see she wouldn't be interested in my internal stock control problems though, so I simply point to where I keep the soul I have, right by the exit, just next to the blues."

— *Nick Hornby*

Character Motivation

I love the way Nick Hornby explains the story goal from the point of view of his main character in High Fidelity.

This man needs balance in his life, and he knows it.

The first story beat pushes him into doing something about it.

That's what a story almost always does. It forces your hero to change something important about himself.

What You Have So Far

So far in your notebook, you should have some research and ideas about the following:

- What kinds of story situations interest you
- What types of characters fascinate you
- What types of settings you're drawn to
- What genre your story will fall into
- A few *'what if'* ideas

What is a story goal?

A *story goal* drives your story and is the foundation of your hook or story question.

It creates tension and pace in your novel.

By making sure you know your story goal from the beginning, you'll create a novel blueprint that works.

Your reader should be desperate to know what the answer to the question will be and won't expect it to be answered until the last act.

A story is about relationships and trouble. A story goal is the force that pushes your MC forward.

It's the reason your MC has to deal with the relationships and troubles she encounters.

A story goal is specific and clear; it's not a general or abstract concept.

Even the MC in a literary novel will have a specific goal.

Deciding now what *specific* goal your Hero wants to achieve will help you develop a story that works.

This is because all the relationships and trouble your Hero has to deal with will be related to this goal.

Knowing your goal early on will help you design a great plot and outline your book with ease.

As I mentioned, it's best to use specific goals rather than general ones.

In *Gone Girl*, for example, Amy wants her unfaithful husband, Nick, to be convicted of her murder.

The story goal therefore is this question:

Will Amy succeed in getting Nick convicted of murdering his own wife?

Simple Ways to Discover Your Story Goal

Have a look over the 'what if?' notes you made in the research section.

Let's say you decide to write a crime story about our elderly bank robber and her plan to steal the crown jewels.

But what does she really want—specifically?

What would drive someone of her age to undertake such a crime?

Here are a few ideas:

1.) She wants enough money to be able to afford to move to a Florida retirement community.

In this instance, the story goal would be: 'Will [retired bank robber] ever move to the retirement village of her dreams?'

2.) She wants to save her 40-year marriage by impressing her gangster husband.

In this case, the story goal could be: 'Will [retired bank robber] save her marriage?'

3.) She needs the money to pay off her grandson's drug debts.

So, the story goal here might be: 'Will [elderly bank robber] save her grandson from a ruthless gang of drug dealers?'

4.) She wants to give the proceeds to an animal charity.

Here the story goal might be: 'Will [retired bank robber] save an animal sanctuary from closing down?

5.) She wants to commit the crime of the century before she dies.

The story goal is probably: 'Will [retired bank robber] become the most notorious thief of all time?'

CAN YOU SEE HOW WHAT THE CHARACTER WANTS TO DO CAN BE TURNED EASILY INTO YOUR STORY QUESTION?

Human beings never work in a vacuum.

We want things for a specific reason, and when you know your story goal, you have the spark of your entire novel in one short sentence.

It's worth spending time working on this one, small sentence.

Once you have it, you'll have a good basis for creating characters.

FROM YOUR NOTES IN THE PREVIOUS SECTION, FIND YOUR CHOSEN 'WHAT IF?' IDEA.

NOW DEVELOP IT INTO A GENRE-RELEVANT AND SPECIFIC STORY GOAL FOR YOUR MC. BE PREPARED TO SPEND SOME TIME PLAYING AROUND WITH YOUR STORY GOAL SENTENCE. IT HAS TO BE BELIEVABLE, CHALLENGING AND YET SOMEHOW ATTAINABLE.

Right, now you have the story seedling. Let's move on to character development.

Chapter Six

CHARACTERS

"I am not an angel," I asserted; "and I will not be one till I die: I will be myself. Mr. Rochester, you must neither expect nor exact anything celestial of me - for you will not get it, any more than I shall get it of you: which I do not at all anticipate."

— *Charlotte Bronte.*

STORY PEOPLE: WHO IS YOUR STORY ABOUT?

Remember, at the beginning, we talked about what a story is. Here's a reminder:

A story is about *relationship*s and *trouble*.

IF YOU HAVEN'T DONE THIS ALREADY, THINK OF A WORKING TITLE FOR YOUR BOOK. TO DO THIS, WRITE A LIST OF 10 IDEAS. YOU MIGHT NOT LIKE ANY OF THEM, BUT PICK ONE.

This is your *working* title. You can always change it later.

YOUR CAST OF CHARACTERS

Threads of connection join each of your characters and link them to the plot.

Think about exploring these bonds between each of your major characters.

Pair them up in different combinations.

Do they like or loathe each other?

Is one of them secretly in love with the other?

Planning to kill the other?

Wanting to steal something from the other?

This is exactly what will happen when you start to write scenes with various members of your cast relating and reacting, often according to who they are with.

Make sure there is a possibility of conflict between each pair so that when they're in a scene together, you know what might cause trouble - even if they're friends.

WRITE DOWN ANY IDEAS FOR CHARACTERS YOU HAVE SO FAR:

OBSTACLES FOR YOUR CHARACTERS TO OVERCOME

Now you have a genre and a title.

To expand on this, we could say that a story is about the suffering of one or more characters and how they overcome (or don't overcome) this suffering.

We could dive even deeper into this.

Let's imagine we're explaining what a story is to an alien who comes from a planet without such things.

In that case, we could tell him that a story is about the way characters struggle to overcome internal and external obstacles.

Internal struggles are things such as the following:

- A desire to be loved
- A lack of courage
- A desire for justice
- A need to overcome grief
- A lust for power
- A hatred of evil
- A need to mature
- Loss of faith in one's god/gods/philosophical system

External struggles are things such as the following:

- Family/cultural disapproval
- Religious disapproval
- Financial disaster
- Environmental issues, for example, earthquake, snowstorm or any other hostile natural conditions
- Someone else's needs and desires

When you choose the internal and external struggles of your MC, you've already begun to make your story people.

There is room, even in a fairly short novella, to explore as many of the above as you like.

The more conflict there is, the more interesting your novel will be, whatever the genre.

MAKE NOTES ON THE KIND OF INTERNAL AND EXTERNAL STRUGGLES YOU'D LIKE TO WRITE ABOUT.

Characters are the heart of your story.

Your characters don't have to be human.

In the novel, *Watership Down*, a group of rabbits struggle against enormous odds to survive.

This is anthropomorphism of course, and entirely valid. In this book, the reader is in no doubt that the rabbits think and feel in human ways.

There are many books out there on the subject of creating characters.

It's a huge subject in novel writing, and rightly so because without interesting, believable story people, your book won't grip your readers.

You might want to start by using a character checklist, and many authors do this.

A checklist includes things such as eye colour, age, favourite food, educational level, shoe size, alcohol consumption and so on.

In my personal experience, these lists are next to useless.

As you write your story, the characters come alive, not the other way round. And there is a far easier way of doing it.

The most important thing to think about when you're developing your characters is what roles they will play in the story.

And how each person is different from one another.

EASY CHARACTER BUILDING

It's easy to build a character once you know how.

I've found that most authors develop their own way of doing this, but we'll start with a simple method to get your characters ready to start living inside the plot of your story.

What about character lists?

As I've said, I'm not a big fan of these, but if you like to use them then go ahead. It's your writing process.

A lot of writing books and websites have examples of character questionnaires.

They include things such as what your character does in her spare time, favourite colour, work history and so on. If you find them useful, add them to your writing process.

I have found they can become dry exercises for many students of novel writing. In my own writing, I like to grow a character on the page.

So, Instead of getting bogged down in useless details you probably won't use, I suggest you begin with a simple character sketch.

Start with a simple sketch.

In *A Game of Thrones*, George R. R. Martin describes two important characters, Jon Snow, the bastard son of the Lord of Winterfell and his half-brother, Robb Stark, through the eyes of their younger brother Bran like this:

> He {Jon Snow} was of an age with Robb, but they did not look alike. Jon was slender, where Robb was muscular, dark where Robb was fair, graceful and quick where his half-brother was strong and fast.

This gives the reader a framework upon which to build a neat visual image of the two brothers.

As it turns out, in this book, Robb Stark becomes King of the North as the battle for the Iron Throne is fought.

For many readers however, John Snow is the true King of the people of the north.

WRITE A SIMPLE SKETCH OF A CHARACTER YOU THINK MIGHT BE YOUR MC. WRITE FROM THE POINT OF VIEW OF ANOTHER CHARACTER.

As the writer, you might like to start by casting for characters, as if you were making a movie.

CASTING FOR THE ROLE

Imagine you are a film director.

You have to cast actors for the roles of the characters in your book.

The easiest way for you as a writer to do this is to search for them on the Internet.

Let's use an elderly computer hacking criminal as an example.

I like to think about the role an actor has played, as well as their looks.

In this case, my chosen character lookalike is Sigourney Weaver, as she appeared playing the part of Dr Grace Augustine in the movie *Avatar*.

Although my MC is much older than Grace, in this futuristic tale, people don't age so fast. I like the tough yet compassionate personality of Grace, so I'll work this into my criminal's overall personality.

WHAT ACTOR MIGHT PLAY YOUR MC?

Backstory: How much do you need?

I think it's helpful to know a few details about the major characters' backstory.

You can go into as much detail as you like, although once again, don't get bogged down by this phase of story development.

TO GET AN IDEA OF WHO YOUR MC IS, THINK ABOUT WHAT MIGHT HAVE CAUSED HER TO END UP WITH HER STORY GOAL.

In our working example of the computer-hacking grandmother, I've decided the reason she is so desperate to go to Trappist 5 is because of what happened to her father.

He was a happy-go-lucky career criminal who ended his life in jail.

I'll dig deeper into this and create a deathbed scene in my mind.

My MC visits him in the dingy prison hospital. Her father tells her he has hated the last 10 years of his life.

Prison has made him cynical, bored and desperately disappointed.

He talks about his dreams of what his last years might have been. He begs her not to end up like him.

This is powerful stuff.

I can then add in a submissive, mousy mother who died alone in her grotty apartment, and whose body was not found for two weeks.

I also know that if my MC has a grandson, she must also be a mother.

I can sketch out a basic life for her.

She was happily married to a salesman and had one child, a daughter.

The husband left her when she went to prison for computer hacking 40 years ago. Since she left jail a decade ago, she's had a string of young lovers.

Her daughter and son-in-law live on the colony of Mars.

That's all I need for now.

NAMING YOUR CHARACTERS

Choosing names is fun.

Make sure they fit the era and genre of your novel.

A regency romance will be ruined if you name your heroine Wendy. It just wasn't a name that existed in the England of the 1830s.

I like to pick names that mean something relevant to my character's personality.

For our example novel, *Trappist 5*, I'll give my MC the name Paradox Lee.

This will remind me (and the reader) that she's a woman of contradictions.

On the surface, she looks much like any other grandmother of 95 in the year 2370. But her dark past as a criminal and ex-con provides a real contrast.

When you're picking names, there are two important points to remember:

- Always choose names that begin with different letters of the alphabet. It's confusing for your reader if you have a Sam, a Sandy and a Steve.
- Always call your character by the same name. If everyone calls her by her nickname, then use that nickname every time you refer to her.

MAKE A LIST OF NAMES FOR AROUND 5 DIFFERENT CHARACTERS IN YOUR NOVEL:

ARCHETYPES/ROLES

Here are some of the character roles you'll need to work with in your novel.

- **Hero, Main Character or Protagonist**: This is the person whose story goal drives the story.
- **Villain, Antagonist or Shadow:** This is the person who stands in the way of your MC achieving her goal. In our example novel, *Trappist 5*, this role is taken by the security officer guarding the jewels on the spaceship.

- **Hero's Sidekick**: This is someone who is loyal to the MC. This person will always stand by the decisions of your MC and go to the ends of earth for them. In *Lord of the Rings*, Frodo's sidekick is Samwise Gamgee. In our example novel, the MC's sidekick is her grandson.
- **Mentor:** For the mentor character type, think of Gandalf or even Haymitch from The Hunger Games. A mentor character is usually older and wiser than your MC. They serve as guides and give advice.
- **Love Interest/Catalyst:** It's always nice to have a romance subplot in any story. In the case of our example novel, I think it would be fun to have a growing romance between the crusty old security officer and Paradox, the criminal.

CHOOSE A NAME FROM YOUR NAME LIST FOR EACH OF THE MAJOR CHARACTER ROLES IN YOUR STORY:

CHARACTER PERSONALITY TYPES OR STYLES

Make sure your major characters have different styles.

This will help with conflict later on.

The single worst mistake a writer can make when it comes to character is to make every person in a novel speak, think and act the same.

Knowing about and working with personality types is one way to avoid this pitfall.

When I studied personality theory, I noticed that most of them boiled down to four essential types: warrior, leader, thinker and relator.

A warrior will find the thinker annoying.

A leader will get frustrated at the sensuality and caring nature of the relator.

Below are these four types I use as springboards to create believable characters and assess possible sources of conflict between them.

Warrior

Confident and quick witted, this type will always fight for what they believe in.

Think of Sigourney Weaver in *Alien,* or Bruce Willis in *Die Hard*.

Leader

This is the decision maker who likes to be in charge and is ambitious and driven.

Think of Elizabeth Bennett in *Pride and Prejudice*, played by Jennifer Ehle, or Harrison Ford in *Indiana Jones.*

Relator

This type likes to be around other people and is loving, loyal, supportive and encouraging.

Think of Rooney Mara in the film *Carol*, or Samwise Gamgee in *Lord of the Rings*.

Thinker/Magician

Aloof and often introverted, this type sees patterns and makes connections.

Think of Amy Dunne in *Gone Girl*, Dr Who in the TV series, *Dr Who*.

THINK ABOUT YOUR MC. GIVE THIS PERSON A GENDER, AN AGE AND A ROLE, ACTIVITY OR JOB.

CHOOSE A PERSONALITY TYPE. NOW GIVE HIM OR HER A NAME. [FOR EXAMPLE: A GIRL OF 16 WHO HUNTS TO FEED HER FAMILY. (KATNISS EVERDEEN FROM THE HUNGER GAMES)] MAKE SOME NOTES OF ANYTHING THAT COMES TO MIND. NO MORE THAN A PAGE.

NOW GIVE YOUR MC A PERSONALITY TYPE. [E.G. KATNISS IS NOT A RELATOR TYPE, ALTHOUGH SHE CARES VERY MUCH FOR THOSE CLOSEST TO HER AS WELL AS THE WEAK AND VULNERABLE. SHE'S A COMPASSIONATE WARRIOR TYPE WHO INSPIRES A REVOLUTION.]

So, now you have: 'A Warrior girl of 16, who hunts to feed her family.'

You could also pinpoint your MC's main internal struggle. [e.g. Katniss needs to overcome the fact that she's not good with people in order to find love.]

In our example novel, Paradox Lee is a woman of 95 (people age more slowly in the future, but she's still pretty old) and an ex-con.

She has lost the last of her money trying to find a cure for her dying grandson.

She is a Leader type, who went to prison to protect a weaker person.

NEXT, WRITE ABOUT YOUR SHADOW OR VILLAIN CHARACTER.

This character is often a similar personality type to your Hero. [e.g. President Snow in *The Hunger Games* is more of a Warrior than a true Leader. He fights to get what he wants and kills his enemies.

Katniss could easily go the same way as her power and influence grow. It's her compassion that makes her the Hero.

Darth Vader is Luke Skywalker's father, a twisted reflection of who Luke might become if he chooses to go over to the Dark Side! Incidentally, they are both Leader types.

MOVING ON, MAKE A LIST OF THE OTHER CHARACTERS YOU'LL NEED TO MAKE YOUR STORY INTERESTING.

Write short sentences for the other character archetypes, making sure they are different personality types.

If you can, make your antagonist a twisted version of your MC's character type. [For example, in *The Hunger Games*, Katniss has two love interests: Gale, another Warrior, and Peeta, whois a Relator type. These two also fulfil the Sidekick role at various times. Her mentor is Haymitch, who is a damaged Thinker type.

In our example novel, the Koenig who owns the crown jewels is a 10,000-year-old man who is a cynic and hates everybody.

He is also a Leader type like our MC Paradox, but a twisted version of one.

Now you have a genre, a working title and some characters to play with. You're ready to develop the setting.

Chapter Seven

SETTING

> "All brightness was gone, leaving nothing. We stepped out of the tent onto nothing. Sledge and tent were there, Estraven stood beside me, but neither he nor I cast any shadow. There was dull light all around, everywhere. When we walked on the crisp snow no shadow showed the footprint. We left no track. Sledge, tent, himself, myself: nothing else at all. No sun, no sky, no horizon, no world."
>
> —*Ursula Le Guin*

WHERE DOES IT ALL HAPPEN?

Every story takes place in a geographical location.

In fact, to create a powerful story, you'll need more than one distinct setting.

In the book *Room*, by Emma Donoghue, although much of it takes place in one tiny room, there is a clear moment when the narrator, a young child, escapes and enters the outside world for the first time in his short life.

This is an example of 'crossing the threshold'. From one world to another.

When we are in the outlining process of building a story, we'll discover how vitally important the moments are when your characters step into a new location.

By placing such moments at certain strategic points in your story design, you can increase their impact.

This style of story development will keep your reader engaged and curious.

Many authors choose to set their first novel somewhere familiar to them.

This is the easiest choice and helps you to imagine each scene in vivid detail without too much research, if any. However, your story can happen anywhere.

Some stories are dependent on place. If you want a volcano to erupt near the end of your book, you better have your characters near one.

THINK ABOUT YOUR OWN PSYCHO-GEOGRAPHY - THE PLACES YOU KNOW WELL. WHERE DO YOU LIVE? WHAT PLACES HAVE YOU LIVED IN? WHERE WOULD YOU LIKE TO SET YOUR NOVEL?

However, your story can happen anywhere.

Some stories are dependent on place. If you want a volcano to erupt near the end of your book, you better have your characters near one.

If you already have a rough idea of the overall setting, now is the time to pin it down.

By doing this at the beginning of your novel writing process, you'll also be able to work out the tone of your novel.

This will enable you to make an outline that suits the type of story you want to tell right from the start.

The more you prepare in the prewriting phase, the less time you'll have to spend editing and rewriting later.

Later on, as you develop as a writer, you'll be able to spiral back and add in the details you need earlier in the novel without planning it first.

Try to develop this skill as you write your first draft. Most of the time you'll find the outline will change as you write, so be aware of changes that need to be made earlier on in your story.

SETTING HELPS YOU CREATE THE TONE OF YOUR NOVEL.

The tone of your novel will depend on which genre you're writing in. A gentle romantic comedy probably won't take place in a dystopian city under siege by dark forces.

However, if you're writing a thriller, then a dystopian city under siege by dark forces is a great setting.

Tone is something you need to set up from the first page of your book. Here are the opening lines of *A Game of Thrones*:

> We should start back,' Gared urged as the woods began to grow dark around them. 'The wildings are dead.'
>
> 'Do the dead frighten you?'

In these two paragraphs, Martin lets the reader know many things.

We know we are in a dark forest. Most fantasy epics will feature natural landscapes, including plenty of trees, and this instantly fulfils reader expectations of the genre.

There is also a sense of impending danger marked by of the use of the word 'dead'.

Interestingly, if you place a power word such as 'dead' at the end of a sentence, it sticks in the reader's mind.

On top of that, there is are already a few hooks or story questions arising in the mind of the reader.

Who or what are the wildings?

Who or what has killed the wildings in the darkening woods?

Why are they dead?

Here's the thing, the entire series of A Song of Ice and Fire, centres around the growing danger presented by the White Walkers.

Spoiler alert: they killed the wildings, and will go on to kill many more so they can create a zombie army from their corpses.

We will look at foreshadowing when you come to create Act 1 of your outline.

For now, it's worth noting that setting can help to do this.

So we've seen that in a very few words, Martin has led us into his fantasy world.

We are aware right from the start that somewhere in the ever-changing landscape of settings, there are dark forests. And they are full of terror and death.

Setting is an excellent way to introduce the tone of your novel right away, so this is the time to think about it within your story-writing process.

World Building

If you haven't been to the place where your story happens, do as much research as you need.

Some authors like to visit locations where their book is set. Others are happy to find out everything they need from the Internet, books, magazines, and so on.

Save any photographs you download or have collected for reference later.

If you're writing about another country, find out about its history, culture, religion, languages, and economy. If you can afford to travel to unfamiliar places that will feature in your book, that's great.

But don't worry if you can't.

WRITE A LIST OF PLACES YOU NEED TO RESEARCH. WHAT DO YOU NEED TO KNOW? IF YOU'RE CREATING WITH A FANTASY WORLD, START SMALL. DESCRIBE ONE SMALL PART OF THE SETTING: AN INN, AN OCEAN, A MOUNTAIN COMMUNITY...

You are a writer, and your imagination is the most important part of your toolkit.

Feed your creativity with whatever you need to make the setting come alive in your mind.

For those of you creating a fantasy, futuristic or science fiction world, make sure you don't get trapped in an endless cycle of world building.

Start with a few basic settings and some ideas about how this world operates, but don't let it go on too long.

WRITE A FEW NOTES FOR A FANTASY/SCIENCE FICTION SETTING:

Your writing process means you decide on a set amount of time for you to spend on this stage.

Many authors stall at this point because they become so fascinated with it that they can't move forward.

Remember, you must ensure you are actively working through the process towards a finished manuscript.

You can't edit and publish something you haven't written.

There are some excellent books on this subject.

I highly recommend Holly Lisle's, *Create a World Clinic*, which covers everything you need to know to make immersive settings in any genre.

THE RELATIONSHIP BETWEEN PACE AND SETTING

Writing a page-turning story your reader can't put down is part of your author craft.

We call this element *pacing*.

Pace is like a wave.

Some scenes are hectic and full of action.

Others are quiet, allowing the reader as well as the characters in the book some breathing space.

Matching your setting to the intended pace of the scene is a great way of keeping your reader's attention.

Quiet scenes are often called 'fireside' scenes.

Action scenes can take place anywhere, but they have a different quality to them. Shorter. Sentences. For one thing.

The landscape or cityscape of your book provides more than just a backdrop.

Weather also has an important part to play too. In *A Game of Thrones*, the repetition of the words 'winter is coming' brings a sense of foreboding every time the phrase is mentioned.

WRITE DOWN IDEAS FOR A GEOGRAPHICAL PLACE/SEASON OR OTHER ENVIRONMENTAL FACTOR WHICH CAN ACT AS A METAPHOR IN YOUR STORY:

Remember, setting is another character in your story.

Make sure yours is fully fleshed out, vibrant and alive with sensual details in your own mind before you begin outlining.

Create as many settings as you can within your story world. In a city, there will be:

- cafés,
- downtown bars,
- upmarket shopping malls,
- crack dens,
- expensive apartments,
- slums,
- museums,
- places of worship,
- city parks and playgrounds.

In a fantasy or historical novel, you might have:

- an inn,
- a castle,
- a dark wood,
- a high mountain,
- a shanty town,
- a smithy,
- a brothel,
- a drinking den,
- a dungeon.

There is no limit really. The more you move your characters around, the greater the sense of movement in your story.

WRITE A LIST OF TYPES OF SETTINGS WITHIN YOUR NOVEL'S WORLD [E.G. CAFES, DUNGEONS, SLEAZY APARTMENT TOWERS, FORESTS, PARKING LOTS ETC]

Beware the 'sitting in the kitchen having a coffee' scene.
Many writers place their quiet or fireside scenes in the kitchen.

The characters drink coffee or tea or even some wine. They have a chat.

This was the biggest mistake I made when I first started writing novels. Many of my scenes happened in a kitchen and involved a couple of people chatting whilst having a drink and smoking endless cigarettes.

It was very French theatre.

But why do this?

Most kitchens do not add much to a reader's vision of your world unless it's a galley in the centre of a spaceship under fire.

Why don't you take your characters out in the woods, on top of a skyscraper or down into the dusty basement?

What about making them talk in a busy café or in the lift on their way to the top floor where an action is about to take place?

MOST OF YOUR BEST IDEAS FOR SETTING WILL HAPPEN AS YOU WRITE.

Creating a world doesn't have to take a lot of time.

Sketch out a few ideas about era, weather and landscape for now, and trust the details will emerge as you do the writing.

MAKE A LIST OF FIVE OR SIX ALTERNATIVE SETTINGS WITHIN YOUR BOOK.

You don't need to go into great detail.

Just think about what kinds of settings you might need to develop the story goal.

For our novel about the elderly criminal and the crown jewels, I made a list like this:

- Viewing deck on large commercial space cruiser, the *Astroterre*
- Interior of the passenger safety deposit vault (where the crown jewels of the Koenig of Andromeda are locked up)
- Escape shuttle.
- Landing dock on the *Astroterre*
- Dining area of the *Astroterre*
- Cheap cabin of the *Astroterre*

CHOOSE ONE PLACE FOR A FIRESIDE SCENE.

This will give you a feel for where your major characters might have their first quiet chat.

Example: I came up with a further setting for this: The virtual reality beachfront café on *Astroterre*.

Create sensory details.

Take one of your chosen settings and decide what kind of sense details your characters might be able to perceive.

Include all the senses: sight, sound, touch, smell and taste. For example, the virtual reality beachfront café includes a turquoise fake ocean, sound of waves, sand between toes, scent of salt in the air con and taste of strawberry ice cream and bad coffee.

Good. Let's get on. You are ready to design your story outline.

Part Two

OUTLINING

PREMISE

"It is my ambition to say in ten sentences what others say in a whole book."

— *Friedrich Nietzsche*

Creating Your Premise Pie

A premise is a succinct summary, an overview of the shape of your story.

So far, you've chosen a genre, done some basic research, made up a story goal question and made a list of major characters and settings.

Now the magic begins.

We're going to combine all these elements and come up with something that sounds like a story.

Time to make a premise pie.

When you've created a story premise, you'll have the core of your plot.

From this point on, you can grow all your ideas into a full-fledged outline.

A story premise includes the following elements:

- Your MC
- A few of her attributes
- A story trigger or setup
- The opposing force or antagonist
- Your story goal
- Main conflict/obstacle to overcome
- The sidekick

The Premise for *A Game of Thrones* (Book One in the Series, *A Song of Ice and Fire*)

First let's study the premise for the bestselling novel by George R.R. Martin. It goes something like this:

> Warden of the North, the loyal Ned Stark, who wants nothing more than to enjoy his home and hearth during the coming winter, hears that the heir to the Iron Throne, the deposed Dragon King and his sister, have come of age, leaving it to Ned to work with King Robert to overcome all who would take the throne by force.

Can you see how this paragraph captures everything the author needed to know to get started on his 700-page fantasy epic?

It doesn't matter what you're writing, from sweet romance to a literary novel of ideas, if you follow these steps you'll save yourself time, effort and thousands of wasted words by working on a strong story premise at this stage in your writing process.

The Premise for Our Example Story

Okay, so let's cook up a workable premise for the example work-in-progress.

This is the science fiction novel about the elderly criminal who looks a bit like Sigourney Weaver in Avatar.

After working on my lists for the settings of this book, I decided to stick with the working title: *Trappist 5*. So, the main elements for the premise of *Trappist 5* will be something like this:

- A broken virtual reality systems designer/criminal hacker who is about to retire (the MC - she's broken because she's lost all her money, her partner and is about to lose her grandson).
- She is an intelligent, confident elderly woman who has done time in jail (a couple of her attributes).
- She discovers a fortune in jewels is travelling aboard the passenger space cruiser she's on (story trigger or set-up).
- The mysterious alien Koenig of Trappist 5 and his armed guard (the antagonist).
- Move to the retirement world of her dreams, Kadia 3 (story goal).
- The Trappist 5 guards are the most vicious, psychological fighting machines in the cosmos (main conflict/obstacle to overcome).
- Teams up with a warrior on the run (sidekick character).

Armed with these ideas, I'll create a single paragraph.

This paragraph will be the premise—the backbone of the entire story:

> Having stumbled on the fact that the space cruiser she's travelling on is carrying the famous crown jewels of a mysterious alien king, an ageing systems analyst who has done time for hacker-theft in the past, and dreams of spending her last years in the expensive community of Kadia 3, joins up with an ex-marine on the run to defeat the King's deadly mind-warrior guards, crack the security code and steal the jewels.

This is all I need to begin outlining my novel. The best thing is that it has built on everything I've done so far, and the process has only taken a few days to create from start to finish.

MAKE YOUR STORY PREMISE. THIS IS A FUN EXERCISE, SO PLAY AROUND WITH THE ELEMENTS UNTIL YOU HAVE SOMETHING YOU LIKE. START BY MAKING A ROUGH LIST OF THE SIX ESSENTIAL ELEMENTS: THE MC, SOME OF HER ATTRIBUTES, A STORY TRIGGER, THE ANTAGONIST, THE MC'S STORY GOAL, MAIN CONFLICT AND THE MC'S SIDEKICK. WHEN YOU'VE MADE YOUR LIST, COMBINE EVERYTHING INTO A SINGLE PARAGRAPH. THIS IS YOUR STORY PREMISE. IT FORMS THE MOLTEN CORE WHICH IGNITES EVERY SCENE OF YOUR STORY. PRINT IT OUT/WRITE IT DOWN AND DISPLAY IT PROMINENTLY. MAKE SURE YOU CAN SEE IT WHENEVER YOU SIT DOWN TO WORK ON YOUR NOVEL.

Chapter Nine

OUTLINING OVERVIEW

"Writing has nothing to do with meaning. It has to do with landsurveying and cartography, including the mapping of countries yet to come."

— *Gilles Deleuze*

What's the point of an outline?

Put simply, an outline is a map of somewhere which does not yet exist. Your story. In the *Novel Writing Blueprint Workbook*, I'm offering you a comprehensive method for writing novels.

Over time, and after a couple of books written using the blueprint, you'll be able to personalise this way of doing things to create your own writing process.

To begin with, I suggest you use the system as it is presented step by step.

In fact, it's best if you use it to develop a new novel. This will give you the chance to test the blueprint and see how it works.

Think of it as a practise piece.

As you go along, you may well find other ways of doing things.

In essence, the blueprint gives you a framework you can play around with to suit your own writing life.

Most authors agree that an outline will help you write your novel faster and smarter.

It means you've tested the story before you commit a single word to the page.

For those of you who have never outlined before, I suggest you try it with an open mind.

Think of it this way: You might enjoy listening to music. You've listened to the music you love all your life. You may even have done some singing or learned to play a simple instrument. But that doesn't mean you're ready to embark on a career as a singer-songwriter who can pull in a paying crowd.

This is the same with writing novels. It's one thing to enjoy reading or writing stories your family and school teachers praised.

But writing a novel to sell to the public takes a bit of study, know-how and practise.

If you want to write, publish and sell your work, you have to develop a good technique.

Outlining a novel is an incredibly powerful way of taking your writing technique to the next level, but if you can't wait to start writing, then blast through a first draft using your story premise alone.

When you've finished, you might want to create an outline during the editing process.

However, I urge you to outline at this point.

If you do, you'll decrease the time you spend rewriting and editing.

I know, because I've tried writing by the seat of my pants, and I ended up having to throw away hundreds of thousands of words.

Just saying.

AN OVERVIEW OF THE OUTLINING METHOD

After many years of studying and teaching writing, it seems to me that a story has four acts.

You might have learned that there are three.

This is true.

But the second act is often divided in two. Act 2A and Act 2B. For the sake of ease, we'll take this split in the second act, and make it into the separate story sections it represents.

ACT ONE: INITIATION

Act 1, which I like to call the **Initiation,** is sometimes called the **Setup**.

In this act, you introduce your major characters, the story goal and the main conflict.

Your hero may or may not be reluctant to get involved. In most crime stories, the hero wants to solve the crime so he chooses to start the story journey willingly—others, not so much. Ned Stark does not want to be Hand of the King, he knows it's a dangerous position and it takes him far from his home and family.

Act one contains plenty of foreshadowing, where you hint at the conflict to come.

Often, in a romance story, one or both of the main characters holds back from love for one reason or another. People do not always want to dive into the adventure ahead.

THRESHOLD 1:

After your hero crosses the first threshold, around a quarter of the way through your story, he enters a new aspect of the story world.

Some people say this is where the story really begins.

This threshold, like all of them, is a liminal place. A no man's land where decisions are crucial.

Your hero will always be forced to choose something here and then deal with the results of that choice.

ACT TWO: RESPONSE

Act 2, sometimes called the **Response,** is when your MC is in a stare of confusion, reacting to everything around him but not understanding the true nature of the forces pushing against him.

During this part of the story, your MC is reacting to events without a clue as to how to overcome them.

This leads to confusion and tension within the MC.

THRESHOLD 2:

This is sometimes called the midpoint crisis.

Often this is when your MC discovers a useful piece of information or does a bit of soul-searching.

ACT THREE: BATTLE

Act 3 is the **Battle**.

This is when the clouds of confusion have begun to clear for your MC.

He knows who his enemies are and has a plan to overcome the obstacles he faces.

There is a saying that this is when your MC enters the Kingdom of Evil.

In other words, there is no turning back.

The MC must fight the antagonist's forces in order to achieve her story goal.

This act ends with the CLIMAX or all-is-lost moment.

THRESHOLD 3:

The all-is-lost moment is exactly what it sounds like. Your reader should be wondering how your MC will overcome it.

Sometimes, he doesn't.

At this point in *A Game of Thrones*, Ned Stark is suffering in prison, in fear for his life.

ACT FOUR: SACRIFICE

Act Four is often referred to as the **Sacrifice** or simply the **Ending**.

To put it simply, your MC must make a life or death decision involving some kind of self-sacrifice.

This is what makes a hero.

It doesn't have to be a real death. Although sometimes it is.

It could be the death of a dream, a relationship or a long-held belief.

Of course, your hero might actually die although usually she does not, but she is prepared to give up something important in order to overcome her inner lack, flaw or misbelief.

Ned Stark chooses to admit to treason in order to save his family.

This ends badly for him, but without his willingness to face some kind of death, it would not be such a powerful story.

He loses his head trying to save his family.

As you develop your own novel writing process, you'll know how much or how little you need to work on your outline.

Some writers jot down a sentence or two for each story 'beat' in the four act structure, and then get on with the first draft.

Others will make detailed notes for every switch and turn in each scene.

The only way to find out what works best for you is to try both ways, or at the very least, create a scene list on notecards which is somewhere in the middle of the two approaches to outlining.

Sometimes I outline, and sometimes I don't. If I do, I make brief notes on a scene for each story beat.

This gives me plenty of wriggle room while at the same time I know I've smoothed out the story architecture before committing to thousands of words.

That's a brief look at what an outline is - which means you're ready to go on to build your story outline

Chapter Ten

INITIAL OUTLINE SKETCH

"I always work from an outline, so I know all of the broad events and some of the finer details before I begin writing the book."

— *Mercedes Lackey*

Your Initial Outline Sketch

This is where you plan the start and end of your story journey.

Where is your story going?

Believe it or not, the best way to develop a strong story outline is to work on the ending first.

By doing this, you can work backwards and make everything fit right from the start.

We always know where we're going when we set out on an important journey.

No matter how much of an adventure it all turns out to be, we have a destination in mind.

WRITE DOWN YOUR FAVOURITE ENDING OF A BOOK OR MOVIE YOU ENJOYED RECENTLY. WHAT HAPPENED AND WHY DID YOU LIKE IT?

When you're clear about the end of your story, you can scatter well-thought-out breadcrumbs throughout the novel for the reader.

It also gives you the opportunity to work in a few misleading scenes or red herrings.

This is what makes outlining so absorbing for the writer.

MAKE BRIEF NOTES ON HOW YOUR STORY WILL END

WHAT DOES YOUR MC WANT TO HAPPEN?

Go back to your story goal.

It should be a clear statement of intent.

Your MC wants to achieve something.

At the start of *A Game of Thrones*, Ned Stark wants his family, the Starks of Winterfell, to endure.

His goal is ensure this happens, no matter what.

At the end of this book, although Ned has lost his head, —his son —Robb Stark—has been proclaimed the King of the North.

So in a way, Ned's wish comes true.

Internal Goals: What the MC Needs for Self-Fulfilment

While there is no doubt that Ned wanted to live out the end of his days at home surrounded by his extended family, he doesn't get what he wants.

Yet in another way, he does.

Robb is at war with those who put Ned to death, but it seems that his family will continue to live at Winterfell.

Ned's sacrifice has not been in vain.

His internal goal is not so much to change but to remain a man of honour and protect his family, just as he always has. This he does.

WHICH OF YOUR MC'S INTERNAL GOALS WILL YOU EMPHASISE AT THE START OF YOUR NOVEL?

External Goals: What the MC Wants in the Outer World

More than anything Ned wants his family to endure.

This wish is granted, despite the rise of the Mother of Dragons in the South, threatening the stability of all the kingdoms, including the Northern lands of Winterfell.

But this is a series, so the author has set up a taster of trouble to come, enticing the reader to read the next book.

WHICH EXTERNAL GOALS [BELONGING TO BOTH THE MC AND THE ANTAGONIST] WILL YOU EXPLORE AT THE START OF YOUR NOVEL?

At the end, your MC gets what he wants or he doesn't.
A happy ending is when he does.
A tragic ending is when he doesn't.

An ambiguous ending is when the reader has to fill in the gaps.

THINKING ABOUT TWISTS AT THE END OF YOUR STORY

You want to make the end of your novel as satisfying to your reader as possible.

In a romance, you have to have a Happy Ever After (HEA) or a Happy For Now (HFN) ending.

In other words, the hero and her love interest should be together.

Without this, it wouldn't be a romance.

But you can work in a great plot twist during the all-is-lost moment at the end of Act 3.

Your job is to make it seem impossible for your star-crossed lovers to get to their HEA/HFN.

Likewise, crime novels work best when the crime is actually solved and the killer revealed.

Here are some ideas for plot twists you might like to consider working in at or near the end of your story:

Identity Twist:

This is when one of your major characters turns out to be someone or something other than they seem to be.

A dear friend is really a vampire.

Darth Vader is Luke Skywalker's father—surprise!

At the end of *A Game of Thrones*, the sister of the heir to the throne turns out to be a Dragon Queen. She cannot be burned by any fire. Oh, and she has three baby dragons to help her fight for the Iron Throne.

And at first she was such a sweet, vulnerable girl . . .

HOW COULD YOU WORK AN IDENTITY TWIST INTO YOUR STORY?

Death Twist:

This is when you kill one of your favourite characters in a

surprising way. George R. R. Martin does this all the time.

It never fails to make his readers desperate, angry and delighted.

WRITE ABOUT A SURPRISE DEATH TWIST YOU COULD ADD TO YOUR STORY?

Motive Twist:

This is when someone is revealed to want the opposite of their professed desire.

A gangster might turn out to be an uncover cop trying to put the gangsters in jail.

A lover might turn to be a con man.

Anyone with a motive might turn out to want the opposite.

WHICH OF YOUR CHARACTERS MIGHT SHOW A MOTIVE TWIST NEAR THE END OF YOUR STORY?

Perception Twist:

It was all a dream . . . but please don't make it all a dream.

That's far too much of a cliché.

However, there are other ways to use this twist.

Perhaps your MC realises her surroundings, desires or goals are not what she thought.

Remember *The Truman Show*?

That kind of thing.

WHAT KIND OF A PERCEPTION TWIST MIGHT THERE BE IN YOUR STORY? IT MIGHT BE SUBTLE OR EXTREME.

Fortune Twist:

This is a twist of fate.

Just when you thought Ned Stark had found a way to survive, well he doesn't.

King Joffrey chops off his head.

You might give a character something at the start of a novel, which is taken away at the end.

It could be anything: a second chance at life, a financial windfall, a house or a lover.

Usually the fortune was given by one character and taken away by another at the end.

WRITE ABOUT A FORTUNE TWIST - GIVEN BY ONE OF YOUR CHARACTERS AND TAKEN AWAY BY ANOTHER AT THE END OF YOUR STORY.

Fulfilment Twist:

What one character gains, another takes away right at the end.

This means that both characters get what they want, but the outcome ends in disaster for one or both of them.

A good example of this is Roald Dahl's story about an abusive husband who plans to murder his wife and bury her in the garden.

As it turns out, she loved him so much she paid for a surprise garden makeover for his birthday, during which his crime is uncovered.

HOW COULD YOU CREATE A LOSE-LOSE SITUATION FOR TWO OF YOUR CHARACTERS? [EVIL CACKLE OF LAUGHTER FROM THE WRITER AS SHE PLANS THIS ONE...]

WHAT HAPPENS TO TRIGGER YOUR STORY?

WHAT EVENT MARKS THE DARKEST MOMENT OF YOUR STORY? MAKE BRIEF NOTES ABOUT THE WORST EVENT OF YOUR MC'S LIFE. IT HAPPENS AROUND THE END OF ACT 3. DISCARD YOUR FIRST FEW IDEAS AND CONTINUE DIGGING DEEP. YOUR AIM IS TO HIT STORY GOLD BY SURPRISING YOURSELF FIRST AND THEN YOUR READERS.

WILL YOU WRITE A TWIST AT THE END? IS IT HAPPY OR SAD OR AMBIGUOUS?

Example: Here's a reminder of the premise for Trappist 5.

> Having stumbled on the fact that the space cruiser she's travelling on is carrying the famous crown jewels of a mysterious alien king, an ageing systems analyst who has done time for hacker-theft in the past, and dreams of spending her last years in the expensive community of Kadia 3, joins up with an ex-marine on the run to defeat the Koenig's deadly mind-bending guards, crack the security code and steal the jewels.

At the beginning I know that my MC, Paradox, discovers the presence of the crown jewels on board the ship.

This triggers her dreams of stealing them - possibly saving her grandson's life and retiring in style.

At the end, I'd like to work in a twist if possible. Quickly, I write a list of a few ideas to discover what I could do:

- She succeeds in freeing her kidnapped grandson but loses her chance to steal the jewels because of this.
- Her grandson dies, but she manages to steal the jewels.
- She frees her grandson and steals the jewels, but her sidekick goes off with the swag.
- She steals the jewels, frees her grandson, but dies on her way to Kadia 3.
- Paradox steals the jewels, rescues her grandson and then has a motive change and gives the proceeds of her crime to the ex-marine for some reason.
- She turns out to be working for the King. She rescues her grandson. The jewels are fakes. Paradox uncovers a criminal network in charge of the King's guard.

- Paradox steals the jewels, rescues her grandson, makes a deal on Mars and gets to Kadia 3 only to find she hates it there . . . finally realising that what she really wants is to live on Mars.
- The grandson is rescued and a cure is found, but the ex-marine dies during the heist, and Paradox realises she loved him.
- The ex-marine turns out to be working for the King.
- The jewels turn out to contain an extremely rare stone among them known as 'Athanasium', which grants the owner immortality but only if the owner keeps it close at all times. The Koenig of Trappist 5 has owned the Athanasium stone for 10,000 years. Unknown to him, there is a group of four 'magician-warrior-teachers' known as The Preceptors, who watch over the stone, moving it on when the time is right. The ex-marine, let's call him, Jorge Morden, is in fact, a Preceptor, charged with ensuring the Athanasium stone ends up with Paradox. [Jorge's storyline features an Identity twist.] Her grandson dies, but she steals the jewels with the help of Jorge. In the end, she sacrifices her dream of moving to Kadia 3. Her destiny is to live for thousands of years and return the stone to Trappist 5 to watch over the time travel machine there. [This gives me an idea for a series. I can call it *Athanasium - The Redstone of Eternity*. It's about the stone as it passes from person to person over the millennia.]

WHAT HAPPENS AT THE BEGINNING OF YOUR STORY? WRITE A NEW LIST OF FIVE OR MORE DIFFERENT IDEAS.

WHAT HAPPENS AT THE END? WRITE A LIST OF 5 OR MORE IDEAS.

Your ideas will become more interesting as you go down the list.

First thoughts will usually be quite general.

Work through until you have something that feels specific, exciting, and original.

Remember, while you're in the planning and writing phase, anything can change.

But it helps to have a good ending to work towards.

IF YOU LIKE DOODLING, OR EVEN IF YOU'VE NEVER DRAWN A THING, TRY MAKING A MAP OF YOUR STORY EVENTS IN YOUR NOTEBOOK.THIS IS JUST AN OVERVIEW SO NO NEED FOR DETAILS, JUST MAKE IT INTERESTING.

Now you should have:

- A story premise

- An outline sketch of your story journey—where your MC starts her journey and where she is at the end

In the next chapter, we'll go back to the beginning and start getting some flesh on them bones.

Chapter Eleven

ACT 1: INITIATION

"There are recurring elements in popularized fairy tales, such as absent parents, some sort of struggle, a transformation, and a marriage. If you look at a range of stories, you find many stories about marriage, sexual initiation, abandonment. The plots often revolve around what to me seem to be elemental fears and desires."

— *Kate Bernheimer*

Act 1: The Initiation

Act 1 is the beginning.

Think of it as a series of initiation rites to get your reader emotionally involved in your story.

Your hero's elemental fears and desires are tested, exposed, and disturbed as she undergoes preparation for the transformation to come.

All major characters are introduced and the spark is lit.

WRITE ABOUT A TIME WHEN YOUR ELEMENTAL FEARS WERE TESTED? HOW MIGHT THIS HELP YOU WRITE AN AUTHENTIC INITIATION OF FEAR FOR YOUR HERO?

Act one has a lot of work to do within roughly 20–25% of your story.

This act launches your reader into the story world, as well as sets up the theme and story goal of your MC.

It also hooks the reader with an overarching story question, and introduces the characters, setting and conflicts.

This is where you can foreshadow things to come.

THEME

Keep your theme simple.

It's the undercurrent working quietly away in the depths of your story.

Sometimes you'll know the theme right from the start, and sometimes it emerges during the writing.

In a romance, for example, the theme is always a version of 'love conquers all'.

A crime novel explores the theme of 'justice' and often looks at some aspect of society such as modern slavery, drug addiction or domestic violence.

In *A Game of Thrones*, the main theme of the whole series is an enquiry into the meaning of power.

Here's a list of possible themes for your book:

- Greed
- Survival
- Jealousy
- Vengeance
- Power
- Love

- Shame
- Pride/Hubris
- Loneliness
- Family
- Secrets
- Justice

In *A Game of Thrones*, the theme of power is tackled by giving different characters different ideas about it.

These books also explore the bonds of family in so many ways.

Example: I'm interested in the primal urge to survive.

What would it mean to be immortal?

I decide that one of my characters might welcome death as a prompt to live as fully as possible.

Another, my MC perhaps, will fear it and be angry about how short life is.

One person will believe in an afterlife, and another will not.

WRITE ABOUT A THEME THAT FASCINATES YOU.

MC's Goal

In *Game of Thrones*, power is the story goal of all the contenders to the Iron Throne.

Some want power so they can harm others.

Some want power because of the wealth it brings.

Some want power because they believe it's their birthright.

Ned Stark is not interested in power for himself.

Slowly we learn his story goal. He wants the powerful position of his House and family to endure, as they have done for many centuries.

His concept of power is that it has to be in the hands of honourable men/women and passed down through family lines.

Notice how Ned's story goal is related to the overall theme of the entire series of AGOT.

MAKE QUICK NOTES ABOUT HOW YOU CAN RELATE YOUR THEME TO YOUR MC'S STORY GOAL.

THE HOOK

Your story should open with a hook.

This will set up the story goal and ignite your reader's desire to find out what happens next.

It took me ages to discover what a story hook is, so don't worry if you haven't sorted this one out in your head yet.

I think I'm a bit slow when it comes to the mechanics of plotting and story weaving, but I'm as determined as a Jack Russell with a stick, so I combed every writing book I could find in order to discover the meaning of this essential widget of story creation.

Here's what I came up with:

Basically, the hook is the main question driving the Antagonistic forces.

If your main antagonist is natural forces i.e. a giant storm, volcanic eruption etc. then think about what might have set it off.

WHAT STORY QUESTION HOOKS YOUR VILLAIN [ANTAGONISTIC FORCES/LOVER]? WRITE ABOUT WHAT DRIVES HIM/HER/IT:

The Hook is different from the Story Goal, because t**he Story Goal relates to the MC's desires.**

By making sure **your Story Goal is in opposition to your main story Hook**, you have created a story with built-in tension.

Which is exactly what you need.

WRITE ABOUT HOW YOUR MC'S STORY GOAL IS IN OPPOSITION TO YOUR VILLAIN'S HOOK [DESIRES]:

Going back to, *A Game of Thrones*, Martin is a master storyteller, so he hooks us straight away with the opening line. Remember how it goes?

'We should get back,' Gared urged as the woods began to grow dark around them. 'The wildings are dead.'

Overarching story question/hook: Who or what killed the wildings?

This hook goes straight into the unconscious mind of the reader.

The hook gradually expands as the series goes on.

After we know what killed the wildings (a sort of ice zombie), we begin to fear for everyone who goes North of the Wall.

Then we learn that there is an entire army of White Walkers (ice zombies), capable of killing every living thing in the entire world.

As Winter takes over this world, the White Walkers move south towards the major cities and populated areas.

So the hook becomes: Will the White Walkers murder every living being in the Seven Kingdoms?

If they are defeated, how will they be defeated?

Interestingly, this boils down to a series of stories about the power of life over death. Of good over evil.

Or the other way round.

Also, as you may have noticed, it opposes Ned Stark's wish that there will always be Starks at Winterfell.

No one but the dead will patrol the walls of Winterfell if the White Walkers prevail.

Example: In my example story, *Trappist 5,* I know the hook must relate to my theme in some way, and be in direct opposition to what my MC wants.

Paradox wants to save her grandson and retire in luxury.

But the Redstone of immortality has to take lives in order to give life. For Paradox to become its next keeper, her grandson must die.

It's a simple equation really. In effect, the Redstone has the ability to bring out the death of all living beings if it falls into the wrong hands.

STORY CONFLICT

In *A Game of Thrones*, the main external conflict is between those who use power for evil and those who wield it for good.

Every character who wants to have power has their own internal conflict over their use of power.

- In a romance novel, the conflict is usually between the two lovers. One or both of them are afraid to love for some reason—internal conflicts. There will also be external conflicts.
- In crime fiction, the conflict is always good versus evil. The murderer represents evil, and the investigator is on the side of good. Of course, this is not always the case, but as I say, go for the simple option if you're new to writing novels.
- In literary fiction, the internal conflict is the main focus. Often this is not resolved and the ending is ambiguous.
- In a thriller, the external conflict is the main focus.

Conflict, Trigger, and Your Opening Scenes

Think of five events to set up your story. I like to think in terms of events rather than scenes.

Remember, a story works because things happen.

You can work in the more static fireside scenes when you know what is happening.

In ACT ONE you'll need the following events:

- **An introductory event**: Bring your MC on stage as soon as possible (two people meet in a romance, a crime is committed in a crime novel etc.). What is your MC doing at the opening of your book? After the prologue, in *A Game of Thrones*, Ned Stark sets out to behead a man who claims to have seen White Walkers.
- **A trigger event**: What changes the direction of your MC's life at this point? In my story, *Trappist 5*, my MC will discover that the priceless jewels are on board the ship.

- **An event that introduces the sidekick**: In my story, I'll introduce the ex-military Jorge Morden. He needs to get Paradox's attention. He also needs her (and the reader) to believe his disguise. So, I think I'll have a scene where she finds him lying on the floor of her cabin, drunk.
- **A new idea event—sometimes called the meeting with the mentor**: The mentor doesn't have to be an older person. Children have a wisdom of their own. I think I'll have a scene where Paradox's 19-year-old grandson, Raze, falls ill and says something wise.
- **An introduction of the antagonist**: In *A Game of Thrones*, the first scene introduces the White Walkers by showing the reader the dead wildings. Further adversaries are introduced when the Lannisters come to Winterfell. I'll introduce death (a major antagonist in my story) in the first scene. After that, I'll have a moment where Paradox bumps into the terrifying mind-torture guards of the Koenig of Trappist 5.

DEVELOP YOUR THEME [THERE IS NO NEED TO SPEND MORE THAN A FEW MINUTES ON THIS PART OF THE DEVELOPMENT PROCESS. AFTER YOU'VE SETTLED ON A GENERAL THEME, THINK OF DIFFERENT WAYS PEOPLE TALK ABOUT IT, AND WRITE A FEW SENTENCES DOWN FROM DIFFERENT SIDES OF THE ARGUMENT.] MULL OVER THE LIST OF THEMES AT THE START OF THIS CHAPTER. THINK OF A FEW OTHERS. WHICH ONE FASCINATES YOU THE MOST? IF YOU'RE WRITING ROMANCE, YOU KNOW YOUR THEME IS LOVE, SO WRITE A PARAGRAPH ABOUT THIS. IF YOU'RE WRITING CRIME FICTION, YOUR THEME IS JUSTICE. WRITE A PARAGRAPH ABOUT THIS. EXPAND ON WHAT YOU WROTE EARLIER:

Example: In my science fiction fantasy novel, I think I'll explore the theme of survival.

I want my reader to ask questions about the meaning of a long life, the reasons we fear death and whether there is any form of an afterlife —technologically based or otherwise.

Could we all be living in a giant computer game?

Is energy ever destroyed?

If it can't be destroyed, what happens to our mind or soul after death?

Is there such a thing as a soul?

Could it be computerised?

Would immortality be a good thing?

What would be the purpose of your life if you knew you could live forever—or at least for a very long time?

In a normal lifespan, how can we make our final years—often plagued by illness and financial struggles—as pleasant as possible?

And so on.

MC'S STORY GOAL

WHAT DOES YOUR MC WANT MORE THAN ANYTHING ELSE? WHAT IS YOUR MC'S ATTITUDE TOWARDS THE THEME? REVISIT YOUR STORY GOAL AND REFINE IT.

In a romance, both MC's want love.

It's their attitude towards it that counts.

Perhaps your MC's attitude towards love might be fearful because he was hurt by someone long ago.

His goal will be to overcome his loneliness.

This gives him a strong inner conflict of desire versus fear.

Do you see how this works? **Theme + Attitude = MC's Goal.**

WRITE OUT THE THEME + ATTITUDE = MC'S STORY GOAL EQUATION FOR YOUR NOVEL:

In my example novel, the theme is 'Survival'.

My MC's attitude towards life is that it ends at death.

There is no afterlife, and she is afraid to die.

Her goal is to live as comfortably as possible in her declining years.

Let's imagine that her sidekick does believe in an afterlife of some kind.

This gives me plenty of scope for conflict as the story unfolds.

The Hook

Look over your story goal.

How can you link this to your theme?

George R. R. Martin links the theme of power to Ned Stark's goal of endurance with honour.

His opening scene is a prologue where Martin shows the reader the deadly power of the White Walkers.

If everyone dies, there will be no houses, no families to endure and no Iron Throne to sit on. All will be lost. The undead White Walkers have no honour, no desire other than death.

Example: *Trappist 5* is a book with the theme of Survival. My MC's goal is: 'Will an elderly retired criminal ever save her grandson and move to the retirement world of her dreams?'

Can you see how this links to the concept of the Redstone of Eternal Life—Athanasium? Good.

A romance story with the theme of love should make sure your star-crossed lovers (they are always star-crossed) meet near the beginning.

If they don't then you should hook your reader by exploring how one of your Main Characters came to have his or her attitude towards love.

In my romance novel Song of the Siren, I spent the first few chapters showing the difficult events of my heroine's early life as the daughter of a witch during the witch trials of 16th century England.

This builds reader sympathy for her and also explains why she believes [falsely] that she will never be worthy of love.

REVISIT YOUR HOOK. WHAT DOES YOUR ANTAGONIST DESIRE? HOW DOES IT RELATE TO THE THEME? THE MORE EVERYTHING RELATES, THE MORE POWERFUL YOUR STORY WILL BE, EVEN IF THE PLOT ITSELF IS FAIRLY SIMPLE.

WRITE A GREAT OPENING LINE OR TWO. WRITE A LIST OF 10 POSSIBLE FIRST LINES FOR YOUR BOOK. THEN CHOOSE ONE THAT HINTS AT THE TONE, THEME AND STORY GOAL OF YOUR STORY. IT DOESN'T HAVE TO BE A COMPLEX, ENCHANTING, BEAUTIFULLY WRITTEN LINE. EDITING COMES LATER. JUST GET SOMETHING DOWN THAT YOU CAN USE AS A SPRINGBOARD FOR AN OPENING SCENE.

Example: I imagine Paradox, an ageing, reformed criminal with plenty of regrets, watching the funeral of a passenger who died during hypersleep.

I wrote out 10 full sentences to open this scene and the story. From my list of 10, I chose one I could work with:

Paradox Lee watched the space funeral with the other passengers from the viewing platform of the cruiser. As the white Morpheus coffin spun out of the airlock into the vastness of infinite space, her spine tingled with a cold dread.

'Her name was Viola. People are saying she didn't die a natural death,' said a voice from behind her.

The hook I want to plant in the reader's mind is something like this: 'Will Paradox survive?'

Or, more likely, 'Who or what killed Viola?' [Answer: the mind-destroying guards of the Redstone. But why? Something to do with theme - death. I think they need to make offerings to the god of death.]

SPEND AN HOUR OR TWO CREATING YOUR ACT 1 OUTLINE.

Make quick notes of possible scenes to launch your story. Make sure things are happening in these scenes. That's why I've called them 'events'.

Make brief notes on the following. 400 words each:

1. AN INTRODUCTORY EVENT/PROLOGUE/INTRODUCE THE MC

2. A TRIGGER EVENT

3. AN EVENT THAT INTRODUCES THE SIDEKICK

4. A NEW IDEA EVENT—SOMETIMES CALLED MEETING THE MENTOR

5. AN INTRODUCTION OF THE ANTAGONIST

You should end up with 9-12 scene ideas.
Next, your MC will cross the first threshold.

Chapter Twelve

THRESHOLD 1: DECISIONS, DECISIONS...

"He had the vague sense of standing on a threshold, the crossing of which would change everything."
—Kate Morton

Threshold 1: Decisions, Decisions . . .

What will make your MC and her sidekick step over the threshold into the juicy middle of a story?

More than that, this is the moment when your MC makes it clear what she is going to do specifically.

In Act 1, you gathered together your major characters.

You've designed a few action scenes to foreshadow the strength of the antagonist.

There has been a trigger event, and you've set up your theme.

Your MC has been wandering in the dark, fire-fighting without a plan, reacting to events, confused about the strength of the antagonist.

However, your MC must grow into an active participant in his or her story.

Readers do not like passive characters who are pushed around by adversity.

When it's time for them to move forward, it's a good idea to **have them make an important decision**.

This makes it look like they jumped into the story and were never pushed.

In crime fiction, the investigator or detective is often already on the case by now.

Nevertheless, she will decide at this point to solve this case, no matter what, usually for personal as well as professional reasons.

In *A Game of Thrones*, at around the 25% mark in the book, Ned Stark has just arrived at Kings Landing.

His wife, Catelyn, has come to the city in secret to give Ned the news that someone tried to murder her and their son in a vicious knife which they barely survived.

She shows Ned the knife, which, as it turns out, belongs to Tyrion Lannister. He is the Queen's brother and a member of a very powerful, and dangerous family.

Ned has two clear choices.

On the one hand, he could throw the knife into the sea and forget the whole thing.

No one would be foolish enough to take on the Lannisters.

On the other hand, he could try to destroy the Lannisters by finding evidence to discredit them.

This is a very dangerous path to take.

What should Ned do?

He stands at the first threshold, ready to make an important decision.

Remember that Ned is a man of honour, and he wishes his house to endure at Winterfell.

Any strike against his wife and son is a threat to what matters most to him.

He knows the Lannisters have no mercy, so he tells his wife to prepare for war.

While she does this, he tells her he will investigate the death of the previous Hand to the King. If he has evidence the Lannisters killed such an important man, he will be able to persuade the King to destroy them.

This choice puts him in conflict with a rich and ruthless opposing family.

What would make your MC decide to jump into the main part of your story?

In a romance, this is often the moment when your two MCs decide to kiss (in a sweet romance), or make passionate, meaningful love (in an erotic romance) for the first time.

They choose to become close, to connect with each other.

WHAT WILL HAPPEN TO MAKE YOUR MC CHOOSE TO GO ON THE REST OF YOUR STORY JOURNEY? WHAT SPECIFIC DECISION WILL SHE MAKE? IN OTHER WORDS, WHAT DOES SHE DECIDE TO DO IN ORDER TO ACHIEVE HER MAIN STORY GOAL? BRAINSTORM SOME IDEAS.

CREATE YOUR THRESHOLD 1 DECISION.

CHECK OUT YOUR MC'S ONE-WORD CHARACTER SUMMARY. WRITE IT DOWN.

In our example story, Paradox has the positive trait of **Determination/Courage.**

She might be an ex-con and a thief, but she never gives up. That's a good thing.

Look back to the ending you've decided on.

The decision your MC makes now will be one step closer to this ending, although it might not be obvious to the reader yet.

In our example story, the ending goes something like this:

Paradox's grandson dies, but she steals the jewels with the help of Jorge. In the end, she sacrifices her dream of moving to Kadia 3.

Her destiny is to live for thousands of years and return the stone to Trappist 5 in order to control the power of death in the universe.

So, we know that Paradox is determined and that she does steal the jewels, including the blood Redstone of Eternal Life, the Athanasium.

Therefore, the choice she makes at Threshold 1 must be to steal the jewels.

Shortly after the voyage to Mars begins, I've decided that Paradox's grandson falls into a coma.

Now Paradox has two reasons to find a lot of money.

Her immediate problem is that she has no money. She wants to pay for onboard treatment and if possible end her days on Kadia 3.

Despite the dangers, Paradox decides to steal the crown jewels. It's a crazy, dangerous idea.

This catapults her into the main part of the story.

GO AHEAD AND CREATE A DECISION FOR YOUR MC. WRITE DOWN EXACTLY WHAT YOUR MC CHOOSES TO DO.

Chapter Thirteen

ACT 2: RESPONSE

"Crying is all right in its way while it lasts. But you have to stop sooner or later, and then you still have to decide what to do."

—*CS Lewis*

Act 2: The Response

At the end of Act 1, your MC has made a life-changing decision.

She has set out on the road to her final confrontation with the antagonist.

How does the antagonist respond to this decision?

The main work of this section of your story, which is also about 25% of the whole book, is for your MC to figure things out.

She might be on the run, on a voyage to start a new life in the US, learning what it means to be a vampire, starting a new job, falling in love, or trying to solve the mystery.

Whatever it is that she's doing, you, the writer, must make it difficult for her.

You must plunge her into chaos. She will try at least one plan of action and fail. This is called, rather unsurprisingly, a try-fail cycle.

It is important to remember that a story is a person who encounters trouble. If in doubt about what to do next, create more trouble. Make it worse. Then double it!

Show your MC's weakness.

Act 2 is a good time to bring out your hero's weakness.

You should have already decided on her main strength during the character sketch phase of your story blueprint.

A great book with a list of one-word character traits and how to apply them in your writing is *The Positive Trait Thesaurus: A Writer's Guide to Character Attributes*, by Angela Ackerman and Becca Puglisi. I highly recommend all their reference books for writers.

In my example, I've already decided that Paradox is a determined person.

Another way of looking at this is to say that she is resilient. In other words, she has courage. She has a strong moral code, although it doesn't always match the rest of society.

She will have to face her fears to reach her goals. She lives her life on her own terms and has a high level of self-belief. Mentally strong, she does not give up because of one or more failures. She has grit. As it turns out, she went to prison for someone else.

However, her weakness is that she doesn't always think before she acts.

She's low on impulse control! This means I can throw all kinds of trouble at her and she'll make mistakes.

If you show your MC's weakness in Act 2, your readers will wonder if she'll fall at the final fence because of it, increasing the tension and drawing it out right till the end.

Character Arc

Put simply, this is what a character arc is:

Your MC overcomes some internal weakness in order to overcome the final battle or all-is-lost moment.

WHAT IS YOUR MC'S WEAKNESS/MISBELIEF ABOUT HIMSELF OR THE WORLD? WHAT WOULD BE THE WORST THING THAT COULD HAPPEN IN ORDER TO CHALLENGE THIS WEAKNESS?

Create movement in Act 2.

You can do this easily by thinking in terms of these kinds of verbs:

- Planning: What does your MC have to do to achieve his goal?
- Training: What does he need to learn? How does he train? Who trains him:
- Hiding: Who is she hiding from? Does she get caught in her hiding place? Where does she hide?
- Running: Where does he run to? (He might be walking, but it will be because he needs to get away from something or someone.)
- Hurting: What hurts him and why?
- Failing: What does he try to do and why does it fail?
- Analysing: What does she need to analyse? Maps, plans, information.
- Observing: Who or what does she observe? What does he learn?
- Hiring: Who does she recruit, and why?
- Persuading: How does he persuade someone to join his quest?

MAKE THESE VERBS INTO SCENES WHERE SOMETHING HAPPENS.

1. PLANNING: WHAT DOES YOUR MC HAVE TO DO TO ACHIEVE HIS GOAL?

2. TRAINING: WHAT DOES HE NEED TO LEARN? HOW DOES HE TRAIN? WHO TRAINS HIM:

3. HIDING: WHO IS SHE HIDING FROM? DOES SHE GET CAUGHT IN HER HIDING PLACE? WHERE DOES SHE HIDE?

4. RUNNING: WHERE DOES HE RUN TO? (HE MIGHT BE WALKING, BUT IT WILL BE BECAUSE HE NEEDS TO GET AWAY FROM SOMETHING OR SOMEONE.)

5. HURTING: WHAT HURTS HIM AND WHY?

6. FAILING: WHAT DOES HE TRY TO DO AND WHY DOES IT FAIL?

7. ANALYSING: WHAT DOES SHE NEED TO ANALYSE? MAPS, PLANS, INFORMATION.

8. OBSERVING: WHO OR WHAT DOES SHE OBSERVE? WHAT DOES HE LEARN?

9. HIRING: WHO DOES SHE RECRUIT, AND WHY?

10. PERSUADING: HOW DOES HE PERSUADE SOMEONE TO JOIN HIS QUEST?

In the example story, *Trappist 5*, Paradox has to **plan** the theft of the jewels. For this to come about, she will have to **observe** the system used to keep the jewels safe.

While doing this, she might have to **hide** from the Koenig in one scene, perhaps after *recklessly* breaking into his cabin . . . (showing her weakness).

She's **recruited** Jorge because he's the one who told her about the jewels. She has no idea about his real identity.

He's a fighter, so he will probably have to **train** her in some kind of combat that might work against the Koenig's guards. They fight with their minds as well as their bodies, so the training will be hard.

In order to **analyse** the problem properly, she might need to **persuade** one of the guards that she's an undercover systems analyst working for the company who own the space cruiser.

She also might need to **hire** a geek who specialises in breaking and entering.

To fully test her courage, I will give her a phobia, one that will really challenge her.

I like the idea of aquaphobia, the fear of drowning. There could be a scene where the antagonist tries to—**hurt** her.

He telepathically sees her worst fear, and make her think she's drowning.

I'll show how she is capable of deep thinking when it comes to computer systems and code just to give the reader a feel for her capabilities.

GO OVER YOUR NOTES OF ACT 2 ACTION VERB SCENES. ARRANGE THEM IN A SEQUENCE THAT MAKES SENSE.

Chapter Fourteen

THRESHOLD 2: A MOMENT OF REALISATION

"I have seen myself backward."
—*Philip K Dick*

Threshold 2: A Moment of Realisation

Threshold 2 should happen around the middle of your story.

The most important thing to remember is that it's **A Big Moment of Realisation.**

This story beat is often called the 'midpoint crisis'. It's a bit like a *midlife* crisis in many ways. In midlife, a person often makes a lot of changes based on his or her experience so far. On reaching middle age, a person might *wonder what kind of person she is.* In addition, a person often sees *the enormity of the odds against him* ever achieving his life goals.

The midpoint crisis is one of the most important beats in your story.

However, it isn't difficult to create a brilliant midpoint crisis if you understand how to craft one.

Threshold 2—the midpoint crisis—is when your MC moves from reaction to action.

It's almost time for him to take on the worst that the antagonist can throw at him.

If he is to have any chance of **achieving his main story goal**, he will have to make use of his greatest asset from now on.

This asset is whatever you chose as his most **positive character trait**.

REMIND YOURSELF OF YOUR MC'S MOST POSITIVE CHARACTER TRAIT:

As your MC crosses the threshold into Act 3 (this act is sometimes called *The Kingdom of Evil*), his battles, obstacles, or conflicts—both inner and outer—will increase.

At the midpoint, you'll design one to three scenes to push your MC into the Kingdom of Evil.

Without this pivotal story beat, your novel will sag, and the last thing you want is the saggy middle syndrome.

Often, at this point, your MC will be attacked—emotionally, physically or psychologically.

WHAT TYPES OF ATTACK WOULD UPSET YOUR MC THE MOST? REMEMBER HIS WORST FEARS ARE A GOOD PLACE TO START. WRITE THESE DOWN, AND SEE HOW YOU CAN MAKE HIM SUFFER...

Of course, the midpoint doesn't have to occur in the exact middle of the book, but it helps to make it as close to the centre as possible.

Make it clear how and why your MC moves from responding or reacting in Act 2 to the action of fighting back in Act 3.

What might propel your MC to fight back?

Often it happens just after the MC receives some kind of *new information*.

In the romance novel, *Jane Eyre*, at the midpoint Jane discovers, at the altar in her wedding dress, that her husband-to-be is already married . . . to a mad woman who lives in the attic.

That is very bad new information about the man she loves.

WHAT KIND OF NEW INFORMATION MIGHT PROPEL YOUR MC TO FIGHT BACK IN ACT 3?

In *A Game of Thrones*, roughly halfway through (page 370 of a 780-page book), Ned Stark is physically attacked.

He finds out exactly how ruthless the Lannisters can be when they are angry. Jaime Lannister kills all of Ned's men, and Ned is left badly injured.

At this point, Ned is given clear evidence that his enemies will stop at nothing to destroy him and the King he supports.

If King Robert dies, so too will Ned, and his House may not endure —which is his main story goal.

Time is running out for the Starks of Winterfell. Ned feels the cold winds of war drawing in and knows he must redouble his efforts to discredit the Lannisters.

He finally realises the enormity of the odds against him.

As you can see, the drama of the midpoint crisis is a crucial part of your novel writing blueprint.

What is a brilliant midpoint crisis?

In his book, *Write Your Novel from the Middle*, James Scott Bell calls Threshold 2 - the Magical Midpoint Moment. He notes that this is the point where one of two things happen:

- 1. Your MC weighs up **the odds against her** and realises exactly how huge they are.
- 2. Your MC weighs up **what kind of a person he is** and whether he wants to stay the same or change.

Therefore, to craft a brilliant midpoint crisis, all you need to do is make sure you craft a great version of one of the above.

Let's study some examples.

In *A Game of Thrones*, Ned Stark is shown **the odds against him** during the attack on his men.

Earlier on, we saw that Ned's main positive character trait was Honour.

Ned must keep his honour by staying by King Robert's side, but he knows he is risking his life by doing so.

Therefore, he chooses to stay by the side of the King he supports instead of returning to his beloved Winterfell where he would be safe.

In *Jane Eyre* (a novel set in Victorian England where a woman's reputation was about all she had), Jane realises **what kind of a person she is**.

She is not the kind of woman to throw her reputation away and become a fallen woman.

Jane's main positive character trait is her Courage.

Rochester offers her a life of wealth and ease as his mistress. But that will not do.

So, despite her deep love of Rochester, Jane leaves him, which means she becomes effectively homeless and penniless.

Remember, a brilliant midpoint crisis will show your MC facing another choice.

One of them is the easy way out. The other is not. Your MC must choose the difficult road into Act 3.

WRITE DOWN AN EASY WAY OUT OF TROUBLE FOR YOUR MC. AND EXPLORE REASONS WHY HE WON'T TAKE THE EASY WAY...

Example: In our example novel, *Trappist 5*, our MC, Paradox Lee, must face a terrible choice at Threshold 2.

Let's say this is the point where her grandson, still in a coma, is kidnapped.

But who kidnaps him and why?

Perhaps, by the middle of the story, Paradox has become friendly with the Koenig's guards in order to get close to the jewels.

She still doesn't know that one of the crown jewels is the Redstone of Eternal Life, but she knows they are worth a huge amount of money.

Before she left Earth, she spent every penny she had trying to find a cure for her sickly grandson. She is broke. But she has pretended she is wealthy to gain the trust of the guards.

Just before the middle of the book, her beloved grandson is kidnapped by an unknown person.

This person believes she is rich and can pay a high ransom. She goes to her new friend in the Koenig's guard to ask for help.

He grows suspicious of her, and attacks her telepathically. She experiences the telepathically induced sensation of almost drowning.

Remember, we gave her a phobia of drowning, so this will really hit her hard.

Remember, Paradox's goal is primarily survival.

She wants to live out the rest of her years in comfort and style.

She also wants her family to survive and be happy. Her MC trait is Courage.

Threshold 2 will include a scene where Paradox realises the enormity of the odds against her.

- The Koenig's guards seem impossible to overcome, which makes the dream of stealing the crown jewels more out of reach than ever.
- Her sick grandson is missing, and she must pay the ransom.
- She cannot tell the on-board guards about the kidnapping because she knows her grandson would be dead before they find him.

- Her own life is in danger from the suspicious Koenig of Trappist 5, who does not trust her any more.
- The main antagonist is the Koenig of Trappist 5, so he must be involved in the kidnapping in some way. Perhaps he is behind the whole thing in order to test Paradox because he has chosen to pass the Redstone of Eternal Life on to her. But she has to earn it first. Of course, Paradox knows nothing of this.

Can you see how everything here builds on the simple story goal we mapped out at the start of *Novel Writing Blueprint*?

REMIND YOURSELF OF YOUR STORY GOAL. WRITE IT DOWN. HOW CAN THIS BE CHALLENGED AT THIS POINT IN YOUR STORY?

Of course, we must also give Paradox Lee an easy choice.
She could just grab an escape shuttle and bail out.
If she does that, she might live.

But the kidnapper has told her that if she leaves the ship, her grandson will die alone.

Even an unconscious person might be able to hear the loving words spoken to him as he is dying.

Her grandson will die soon anyway, but she doesn't want him to die among strangers.

Besides, she's discovered there is a new treatment which might save her grandson - but it's very expensive.

There is only ONE choice a character like her would make.

That choice is the hard road.

She must turn to face the antagonist and fight back.

Paradox decides that no matter what, she will find a way to steal enough money to free her grandson.

She must find a way to take the crown jewels and sell them on before the clock stops ticking, and her grandson is dead.

And if a single hair on his head has been harmed, she will kill everyone involved in taking him.

But if she is reckless (the shadow quality of Courage), everything will go wrong.

WHAT PROPELS YOUR MC TO CROSS THRESHOLD 2 INTO ACT 3: THE FIGHT BACK.

Go over your notes on the story goal, your MC's main positive character trait and the scene ideas you have so far.

Now think about the worst thing you could do to your MC at this point in her story.

Balance that with notes on the easy way out.

WHAT KINDS OF ODDS ARE STACKED AGAINST YOUR MC?

WHAT KIND OF PERSON DOES HE WANT TO BECOME?

WHAT IS THE SHADOW PERSONALITY TRAIT/WEAKNESS/MISBELIEF/DEEPEST FEAR OF YOUR MC? HOW MIGHT THIS MAKE THINGS EVEN WORSE?

When you've made some notes, look over what you've got.

ORGANISE YOUR IDEAS INTO A SEQUENCE OF ONE TO THREE DIFFERENT SCENES. NOTE THESE SCENES DOWN AND GIVE THEM ONE-SENTENCE NAMES:

Next, your MC will enter Act 3, the Battle. And the fight back begins.

Chapter Fifteen

ACT 3: BATTLE

> "A great battle is a terrible thing," the old knight said, "but in the midst of blood and carnage, there is sometimes also beauty, beauty that could break your heart."
>
> —*George RR Martin*

Act 3: The Fight Back

Act 3 should be fairly easy to outline because you've already set most of the story ideas in motion.

Your novel writing blueprint gives you a process of outlining that works from an initial idea.

The story goal (initial idea) is the initial few pencil lines.

By crafting your ending, the first two acts and two thresholds of your story, you are halfway through your story development.

The most important scene in this act is what is often called the **all-is-lost moment.**

This is when things could go either way, but it really looks as though your MC will lose everything.

Your reader wants the MC to win, but it seems impossible.

In a romance, this is the point when it looks like your lovers will never get together and have their HEA.

Your job as an author is to make sure this moment is worse than anything that has gone on before.

MAKE A LIST OF 10 POSSIBLE IDEAS FOR THE ALL-IS-LOST MOMENT IN YOUR STORY:

You already know how Act 3 will end.

Look back over your notes, and find your list of story endings.

You should have chosen one that strikes you as interesting and original.

When George R. R. Martin was devising *A Game of Thrones*, he knew Ned Stark was going to die at the hands of a sadistic new King.

WRITE DOWN YOUR CHOSEN STORY ENDING OR OUTCOME. WILL YOUR MC GET WHAT SHE WANTS OR NOT? WILL SHE GET IT AND THEN DISCOVER SHE NO LONGER WANTS IT? WILL SHE GET SOMETHING ELSE WHICH IS JUST AS GOOD? OR WILL SHE LOSE HER HEAD?

All he had to do was get Ned up on the podium with the new King and an axeman ready to chop off his head.

I remember the first time I saw this scene on the TV series.

I hadn't read the book then and had no idea what was about to happen.

I wanted Ned to live.

I thought he would get out of it. But he didn't.

The shock of his death made me want to throw something at the TV. Then I went off and read the book.

This is how you want your reader to feel—not that they want to throw something, although they might.

You want to make them root for your MC by hoping against hope that the MC's story goal is achieved.

Now, *A Game of Thrones* is the first in a long series, so Ned's desire for House Stark to endure may well come true in the final book.

However, if you're writing a standalone book, you have to make sure you work towards an ending that satisfies.

Act 3 is the gateway to the ending. It is full of difficulties for your MC.

HOW TO CRAFT A GREAT ACT 3

Once again, Act 3 is around 20–25% of your novel.

By now, you should know how long your story will be in terms of word count.

As a general rule, a novelette is around 7,500 - 17,500, a novella is from 17,600 - 49,000 words and a novel is anything from 50,000 to 120,000 words.

The average full length novel is usually 60,000 - 80,000 words.

So, if you imagine that a scene is between 1,000 and 2,000words, you'll need about 7-10 [or more] scenes for each act depending on how long your scenes turn out to be.

CREATE A WRITING GOAL. WHEN WILL YOUR NOVEL BE FINISHED? WRITE DOWN THE DATE.

Your all-is-lost moment should come close to three quarters of the way through your novel.

A little after this point in *A Game of Thrones*, Ned Stark finds himself in a stinking prison.

King Robert is dead, and a new, terrifyingly barbarous King sits on the throne.

Ned is suspected of treason. If he is found guilty, he will lose his head.

That's about as bad as it can get for anyone. After you know specifically how bad it gets for your MC, you can easily think up the scenes leading up to it.

In our example work-in-progress, *Trappist 5*, Paradox Lee has decided to steal the jewels quickly.

She doesn't have time to wait for a good moment—she has to do it within 24 hours, or her grandson is dead.

She has to use her criminal ability to enter into the virtual world and hack into locked systems.

The biggest risk she'll face is that the Koenig's guards are telepathic.

She doesn't know that the Koenig himself is holding her grandson or that he wants her to take the jewel of eternal life from him.

We'll save this revelation until the last act. So, what is the worst that can happen?

The worst that could happen is that her sidekick, the handsome young Jorge (who is in league with the Koenig), turns her in.

His betrayal means she is locked in a virtual holding cell. Because this is virtual reality, she has to face her worst fear.

Worse than drowning.

It is the loss of her grandson.

Let's say that her mind is trapped on a tiny, dark, virtual island, and a great tidal wave is rushing towards her.

The problem is, if she dies in the virtual world, she'll die in real life.

Her heart is not strong. She's old. Her grandson is relying on her.

Now, we've made it pretty bad for her.

But there's more. We want to make it worse than that.

Let's say she sees faces in the tidal wave as it bears down on her—the face of her grandson calling out for her and the face of the Koenig, mocking her for her recklessness and stupidity.

Remember, we said that recklessness was the shadow or negative side of her trait of Courage.

Having built up this situation scene by scene, we end Act 3 with a situation that looks doomed.

How will she ever get out of this one? All seems very lost indeed.

By now, you might think I've worked this story idea into a corner.

After all I've decided Paradox Lee will survive. She steals the Redstone of Eternal Life, although it's too late for her grandson.

The stone only works on one person at a time, and it has chosen her.

Death must take an offering.

I am now officially in what we might call a deep, dark plot hole. Many years ago, I attended a workshop run by a famous crime writer. She gave a piece of advice I've never forgotten:

> *Every writer can dig themselves out of any plot hole, no matter how deep and dark it might be.*

That is the work of Act 4. For now, we'll leave Paradox there, terrified, alone and with nowhere to run.

WRITE A LIST OF THE WORST THING THAT COULD HAPPEN TO YOUR MC. NOW MAKE IT WORSE . . . AND WORSE STILL. DON'T WORRY IF YOU CAN'T THINK A WAY OUT OF IT YET. IT MUST LOOK LIKE YOUR MC WILL NEVER ACHIEVE HIS OR HER GOAL. WHATEVER GENRE YOU'RE WRITING IN, THE SITUATION LOOKS TOTALLY DOOMED. IT'S REALLY GOOD IF YOU THINK YOU CAN NEVER GET YOUR MC OUT OF THIS HOLE BECAUSE YOUR READER WILL BELIEVE IT TOO.

NOW ORGANISE YOUR SCENES. MAKE A LIST OF SCENES LEADING UP TO THE ALL-IS-LOST MOMENT.

Trust the creativity of your unconscious mind. The answer will emerge from there.

Chapter Sixteen

THRESHOLD 3: A FRIEND IN NEED

"Each friend represents a world in us, a world possibly not born until they arrive."

—Anais Nin

Threshold 3: A friend in need

At this point in the story, your character is going through the worst possible torment so far on his road to attaining his goal.

To make the transition to the final act, you should change the pace of the story now.

Your novel needs a fireside moment.

This will relieve the tension, making way for the increase in tension you'll create in Act 4.

WRITE A LIST OF POSSIBLE SETTINGS FOR YOUR THRESHOLD 3 FIRESIDE MOMENT. MAKE THEM AS INTERESTING AND ORIGINAL AS YOU CAN:

Threshold Guardian

There is an archetype who stands on the threshold between life and death, appearing in many myths and legends from around the world.

Often this guardian throws rocks in the way of the Hero, making the journey even harder than it already was,

In *A Game of Thrones*, Ned Stark waits to hear his fate in the dark, miserable, stinking dungeon.

He thinks about his failure. He wonders whether his honour will save his children.

Then, he has a visitor, an ally who supports the Starks of Winterfell.

The character who visits him in this vile place offers him a solution.

If Ned puts away his pride and admits to treason, he might get away with banishment instead of death. If Ned does this, he will lose his main strength, which is his honour (and might reasonably be interpreted as pride).

It's best not to introduce a new character right now and Martin does not do this.

We know the person who visits Ned.

Any character already present in your story can wear the mask of the threshold guardian.

Look through your character notes.

Who might play this role?

Example: In the example work in progress, Paradox Lee waits for the tidal wave to overcome her.

She believes she will die in virtual reality if the wave engulfs her.

As she stands there, shivering in terror, who might pay her a visit?

In an action sequence like this, it's difficult to halt everything for a quiet fireside chat. Therefore, it's a good place for a flashback.

Anything you think of now can be foreshadowed earlier on in your novel outline.

A threshold guardian is not usually the antagonist himself or herself.

I know that my MC has got to know a few of the Koenig's guards as well as the Preceptor, Jorge.

However, the guards might be a bit too close to the antagonist to play this role.

Paradox thinks Jorge has betrayed her, and she doesn't trust him. That's good.

The threshold guardian has motives the reader doesn't yet understand. In fact, Paradox doesn't know Jorge's true role in the story yet because I've decided he turns out to be someone other than he seems to be at the end.

Yet Paradox has fallen in love with him.

Perhaps he reminds her of a long-lost lover, someone who died in a drowning accident. This person was someone she could not save, even though she tried and almost died in the attempt—hence her fear of water.

I could, in fact, introduce the dead lover earlier on in the story—somewhere in Act 1.

After noodling around in my notebook, I decide the threshold guardian is a virtual reality Jorge, who appears like a drowned man from the ocean around the virtual island upon which Paradox waits in terror for the wave.

This has to be a short conversation as the wall of water draws near.

He tells her this might be a good day to die. All she has to do is submit to the wave as it overcomes her.

After all, her grandson will die soon.

She hasn't stolen the priceless jewels, so all she has ahead of her is a steady decline in health.

She'll live in poverty because her criminal record marks her out on Mars, and she isn't allowed access to any systems with Earth links.

Or she could fight the VR with everything she has. She's an experienced hacker. Nothing in the game is real, so all she has to do is fight VR with VR. What could she imagine that might overcome a wall of water?

Out of Control

Your MC should feel out of control at this point.

She can't turn back the tidal wave of events about to swallow her up.

Yet still, she has to make a choice.

Ned has to choose whether to give up his honour and save his daughters or stand firm in his fight against the Lannisters, risking everything he holds dear.

The choice you give your MC at this point should be equally as difficult.

Example: If Paradox decides to give in to death, she will in effect be abandoning her grandson to die alone.

BACKSTORY AND OVERCOMING FEAR

It's time for your MC to show her true colours.

For her to overcome the all-is-lost moment, she has to overcome her flaw or false belief about herself and what she is capable of.

Certain types of character don't really grow much in a story.

This is where genre is a key element in the way you craft your story.

James Bond, who is the MC in thrillers, does not change. He is brave and resourceful at all times.

If you're writing this kind of story, make sure your MC comes up with a solution to the all-is-lost moment that is interesting, original and relevant to their skills.

I've decided that Paradox does not abandon her grandson or her dreams.

She does not act recklessly, as she has done in the past. Instead, she uses her skills as a virtual hacker to solve the problem.

And this is only possible if she is calm and full of courage.

There is only way to avoid the tidal wave.

Find higher ground or fly.

But it will be horrendously painful.

It takes a lot of courage to break your mind into a thousand pieces as it searches for a thing.

Paradox reaches out into the space cruiser's network, searching for a pair of virtual wings. I have no idea how this works, but this is what she does.

I'll also make sure a small version of this 'reaching out and finding a thing' in the network (and the horrible pain it causes) is demonstrated earlier in the story.

Your MC's Strength

Ned Stark dies because he makes the wrong choice at this point . . . or maybe not.

We'll have a closer look at this in the next section.

For now, let's just say that the choice your character makes at this threshold is based on what type of person he or she is.

Answer the questions below to craft a powerful third threshold.

WHAT IS YOUR MC'S STRENGTH [IT SHOULD BE THE OPPOSITE OF HIS MOST POSITIVE CHARACTER TRAIT], AND HOW DOES IT GET HIM THROUGH THE ALL-IS-LOST MOMENT?

HOW DOES THE THRESHOLD GUARDIAN APPEAR? THE THRESHOLD GUARDIAN CAN BE LIVING OR DEAD. HE OR SHE MIGHT APPEAR IN REALITY OR IN A DREAM, HALLUCINATION OR FLASHBACK.

WHAT CHOICES WILL YOUR MC HAVE? MAKE BOTH CHOICES BAD—THINK OF A ROCK AND A HARD PLACE. WHAT DECISION WILL YOUR MC MAKE?

You've almost finished designing the main scenes of your fledgling story.

Next, you'll discover how to design a thundering final act and the end of your story.

Chapter Seventeen

ACT 4: SACRIFICE

> "Sometimes when you sacrifice something precious, you're not really losing it. You're just passing it on to someone else."
>
> —*Mitch Albom*

Act 4: Sacrifice

Remember how we set up and launched your story? You created the following:

- A theme
- A story goal (your MC's goal)
- The hook or story question - indicating the force opposing your MC's story goal
- Your Act 1: Launch scenes:
- An introductory event/prologue/introduce the MC
- A trigger event

- An event that introduces the sidekick
- A new idea event—sometimes called meeting the mentor
- An introduction to the antagonist

The work of Act 4 is wrapping this all up in a dramatic and satisfying way.

Theme

At the end of a romance, which always has the theme of love, your hero and heroine (hero and hero, heroine and heroine) will declare their love, get married, move in together, buy a house, go on holiday or whatever.

At the end of *A Game of Thrones*, Ned Stark is dead.

However, a new and incredibly powerful contender to the Iron Throne arises.

The last chapter describes how her power is born in blood and fire. Interestingly, the power of fire is the only thing that can overcome the power of ice (the zombie White Walkers have the power of ice).

See how theme brings your book full circle?

Bringing your story to a satisfying end is all about coming full circle.

Make notes about how you can bring each of your Act 1 elements to a satisfactory close in Act 4.

Don't worry if you can't answer each of these questions now, but make sure you can by the time you come to write your first draft.

HOW DO YOU ADD DEPTH TO YOUR THEME BY THE END OF THE BOOK?

YOUR MC'S GOAL - HAS SHE ACHIEVED IT OR NOT? THINK OF SURPRISING WAYS SHE MIGHT HAVE WON, LOST OR CHANGED HER GOALS.

THE HOOK OR STORY QUESTION - INDICATING THE FORCE OPPOSING YOUR MC'S STORY GOAL. DOES THE VILLAIN/ANTAGONIST WIN OR LOSE? HOW? WHY?

AN INTRODUCTORY EVENT - HOW IS THIS ECHOED IN ACT 4?

A TRIGGER EVENT - HOW IS THIS RESOLVED IN ACT 4?

THE SIDEKICK - WHAT HAPPENS TO THIS CHARACTER IN ACT 4?

ADVICE OF THE MENTOR - HOW IS THIS ECHOED OR ACTED UPON IN ACT 4?

THE ANTAGONIST OR VILLAIN - ARE THEY DEAD OR ALIVE BY THE END OF ACT 4?

IN A ROMANCE, THE ANTAGONIST IS ALWAYS THE LOVER, SO IT'S BEST IF THEY LIVE. BUT SOMETHING ELSE HAS TO DIE IN THIS ACT. WHAT DOES YOUR HERO GIVE UP IN ORDER TO GAIN WHAT SHE NEEDS TO GROW?

Example: In *Trappist 5,* I opened the book with a space funeral. I will close it with Paradox Lee laying out the body of her dead grandson.

However, things have changed a lot.

Paradox used to think that death was the end of consciousness.

How can I change that attitude? Simple.

I'll make sure she dies physically in Act 4 and has a near-death experience of some kind, convincing her that her grandson was right all along: nothing ever truly dies.

Your reader doesn't have to agree with your MC's attitude change.

It just has to make them *feel* something.

STORY GOAL

Your MC might not live to the end of your book.

Ned Stark is dead, but his son has been declared the King in the North.

Ned's desire for his family to endure in the North appears to have been fulfilled.

In the end of *Trappist 5,* Paradox Lee is alive, but her grandson is dead.

She manages to free him from the kidnapper, and he dies in her arms.

Remember, I decided that her story goal at the outset was to make enough money to retire in style.

Often your MC's story goal has changed by the end.

Now she has become the keeper of the Redstone of Eternal Life, and she knows she will live for another thousand years or more.

Beyond physical death, she will also survive in some form or another.

Her story goal has changed.

The fear of ageing and death has gone.

She no longer wishes to retire in peace.

She will replace the Koenig, taking up his position on Trappist 5 as the Queen of Fates. It's a difficult job, but someone is always chosen to do it.

HAS YOUR MC'S STORY GOAL CHANGED AT THE END? IF SO, WHAT MIGHT IT BE?

THE HOOK

Remember the hook I threw out in Act 1 of *Trappist 5*? It was: 'Will Paradox survive?' or, more likely, 'Why was Viola killed?'

Right now, I have no idea who Viola was, or why she died, but I know she died at the hands of the Koenig's guards and it had something to do with the Redstone of Eternity.

However, I know I have to make sure this has been cleared up by the final act, if not before.

Perhaps Viola was the loyal daughter of the Koenig.

Maybe he asked her to kill him, but the Redstone took her life instead. Death must have its offering.

The question of Paradox's survival can be answered in the last few paragraphs.

She will survive.

In fact, now her life has changed completely.

Her goal is find a way to live forever, without becoming cynical and cruel like the Koenig she has defeated.

CONFLICT

The last obstacle is a confrontation with the antagonist. In fact, this turns out to be two antagonists: the one inside your MC and the external one in the form of your shadow character.

Ned Stark faces down a man without honour—his shadow self—the evil King Joffrey.

Ned dies a hero's death as he kneels in front of the executioner without a word.

He loses his life, but his family endures.

Example: In *Trappist 5*, Paradox has to face the Koenig. Perhaps he begs her to kill him, but she is a thief not a killer.

She has to overcome her inner conflict to do this.

Her reckless desire to run from conflict, to avoid death if possible, must be put aside.

She realises that the Koenig is much like her, a reckless man who has paid a high price for his careless mistakes.

I can go back to one of the previous acts and create a scene where the Koenig's thoughtless attitude has brought great harm to someone he loved.

This will be a flashback to something that happened when he was younger and the reason he has grown cynical and cruel.

A FRIEND IN NEED

At the end of your book, your MC will have a scene where an ally comforts him.

At the end of *A Game of Thrones*, Ned is beheaded in public. In the crowd is Ned's daughter Arya. A friend of Ned's who was introduced earlier in the story rescues Arya before she is captured by the Lannisters.

WHO IS YOUR MC'S FRIEND IN NEED? HOW MIGHT YOU INTRODUCE THEM EARLIER IN THE STORY? IS IT THE SAME ALLY WHO TALKED TO THEM DURING THE ALL-IS-LOST MOMENT? IF THIS PERSON IS THE SIDEKICK, HAVE THEY BEEN WITH THE MC ALL ALONG, OR DO THEY RETURN WITH HELP?

SACRIFICE

No ending is complete without some kind of sacrifice. Something must be given up so the story goal can be gained.

It can be a physical death or something else, such as a job, a dream, a home, and so on.

The sacrifice is based on whatever choice your MC made in Threshold 3.

Ned Stark gives up his life for his honour and his family. His goal that his family will endure is fulfilled but not in the way your reader expected.

What does Paradox give up to gain her story goal?

She gives up her grandson.

She had just discovered a new cure for his terrible disease, but it is too late.

Nothing could have saved him.

Physical death comes to every living being, even the so-called 'gods' who have access to the Redstone of Eternal Life—Athanasium.

She learns that much is lost when we don't have a body to house us, mainly for those left behind.

Her grief is palpable.

BY NOW YOU SHOULD HAVE NOTES ON HOW YOU CAN WRAP UP YOUR STORY BY BRINGING IT FULL CIRCLE. TO RECAP, WRITE DOWN HOW YOU CAN ANSWER THE STORY GOAL AND HOOK:

WHAT WILL HAPPEN WHEN YOUR MC CONFRONTS YOUR ANTAGONIST IN THE FINAL SHOWDOWN?

WHAT PRECIOUS THING WILL YOUR MC SACRIFICE OR GIVE UP IN ORDER TO GAIN SOMETHING ELSE WHICH IS MEANINGFUL?

HOW DOES THIS PRECIOUS THING SHE GAINS RELATE TO THE THEME? IN A ROMANCE, YOUR MC WILL GAIN LOVE, BUT AT WHAT COST? IN A MYSTERY OR THRILLER STORY, THE SACRIFICE IS USUALLY MORE EXTERNAL THAN INTERNAL. THE MC REMAINS THE SAME ON THE INSIDE. THE KILLER IS CAUGHT. JUSTICE IS RESTORED.

USING THE NOTES YOU'VE ALREADY MADE IN THIS CHAPTER, CREATE A LIST OF 7–10 SCENE IDEAS FOR YOUR LAST ACT.

HOW CAN YOU MAKE SURE THAT THE LAST SCENE OR TWO SHOWS HOW THE SACRIFICE HAS CHANGED THE CHARACTERS IN YOUR STORY?

WRITE A LIST OF 10 LAST LINES.

When your reader closes the book, you want him to love your story.

You would like him to read the next book you write.

It's great if your last line can echo something in the opening lines of your story.

In many ways, the ending of a story is the most important part.

If your reader closes the book feeling warm towards you as a writer, they will want to read more or your work.

Craft the best Act 4 you can.

Now, you have a story outline.

Check over it to make sure the story feels right. Is it interesting? Have you covered all the main story beats?

WRITE A LIST OF ALL YOUR MAIN SCENES IN ORDER: ACT 1:

THRESHOLD 1:

ACT 2:

THRESHOLD 2:

ACT 3:

THRESHOLD 3:

ACT 4:

When this is done, you're ready to write the first draft of your novel.

Part Three

FREEWRITING FIRST DRAFT

Chapter Eighteen

PREPARING TO WRITE

"Make the tale live for us
    In all its many bearings,
    O Muse."
    —Homer

Preparing to Write

As we've seen in relation to planning our story, preparation is everything.

You have a strong story outline and are raring to get on with it.

But first, you should think about where, when and how much time you have to write your initial manuscript.

It doesn't take long to get these things in order, so let's get organised.

Where will you write?

When it's time for you to write your novel, you'll need to retreat into a self-styled writing cave.

Many writers star their novel writing career working at the kitchen table, in bed, in the garden shed, on the train or in the café where they always have lunch.

Most of us have jobs to go to, children to care for or any number of a thousand different commitments.

We want to mark out a special territory to write.

WHERE DO YOU PLAN TO WRITE YOUR NOVEL?

Many books recommend creating the perfect writing space.

However, beware of thinking that a nice office or nook is all you need to ensure you get the writing done.

Over the years, I've found the most important element of writing my first draft is not in the outside world. Not at all.

The writing cave is inside you.

I recommend you train yourself to write anywhere.

This is so that you can deal with interruptions of any kind.

For the first few years when I was trying to write, I had a lovely room to write in. It overlooked a beautiful garden. It was peaceful and quiet. The desk was comfortable. I had my reference books around me.

Yet, life kept getting in the way.

I had a family, work and other stuff going on.

I let the distractions stop my writing flow completely.

Like most of us, other things in life needed my attention, and sometimes they took me away from my desk.

And whenever I had to spend a few days, weeks or more dealing with other things, I found I had lost the thread of what I was writing.

Okay, I did start out as a 'pantser' in those days, writing books without a clear outline.

Yet, even when I did get into creating quite lengthy outlines, I still found I had lost my connection with a particular book when I had been away for more than a few days.

This problem only resolved itself when I made a decision that my writing space was inside my own head.

Make a decision here and now to train yourself to write wherever you are.

If you go on holiday, take your outline and a notebook with you.

Even if you only manage a page or two a day, you'll remain in contact with your story.

I have an imaginary cave to retreat into where the writing takes place. It is always with me.

Create one for yourself now, and you'll save a lot time and heartache.

And, by all means, have a corner, studio, room or table where you usually write in the physical world too.

WHEN CAN YOU WRITE? NOTE DOWN DAYS AND TIMES WHEN YOU CAN WRITE. THEN COPY THEM INTO YOUR DIARY OR CALENDAR.

A lot of writers talk about getting up at the crack of dawn to write.
The early morning is not my time.
I like the night.

I wrote my first novel every night after a day at work, when my children were in bed.

However, I also write in the morning—just not at 5 am or whatever.

After I realised the writing cave was within, I also came to understand that it was important to make myself write at any time of the day or night too.

Practice writing whenever you have an hour or more to spare.

Many people say they don't have time to write a novel.

If this is the case, then don't do it!

The reality is, writing a full length novel or even a novella means you need to carve out regular writing time.

Look at your day.

Can you watch less TV?

Go to bed later?

Get up earlier?

Block out writing time in your diary, and turn up at the page. That's all it takes.

Remember this: If you are committed to your creativity, you can find time to write.

HOW LONG WILL IT TAKE TO WRITE YOUR NOVEL?

It depends. Some people take a year or two to write their first book.

If you aim to write a novel in four months, then you could break down your process like this:

- Prewriting phase, including creating your story outline: two to four weeks

- Writing your first draft (this depends a lot on the length of your book): four to eight weeks
- Editing: two to four weeks
- Publishing: If self-publishing, one week for formatting and uploading to distributors such as Amazon, Kobo, Draft2Digital and so on

HOW LONG DO YOU PLAN TO SPEND ON EACH PHASE OF THE NOVEL WRITING PROCESS?

PREWRITING. DATES:

WRITING YOUR FIRST DRAFT. DATES:

EDITING. DATES:

REWRITING? DATES:

PUBLISHING: IF SELF-PUBLISHING, YOU NEED TIME FOR FORMATTING AND UPLOADING TO DISTRIBUTORS SUCH AS AMAZON, KOBO, DRAFT2DIGITAL AND SO ON. DATES:

Remember this:

The more you write and refine your writing process, the quicker you'll get.

Rituals to Get You Writing

I've written a whole book on this.

In essence, like all creative work, writing a novel is a state of mind.

You'll need to reflect on how you feel at each phase of the writing process.

Your novel writing process will improve if you write about your experiences at each stage in a journal.

Most writers do this, often as a warmup before beginning their writing task for the day.

Rituals are a useful way of entering your 'writing cave'.

To step over the threshold into the right state of mind, turn off all distractions, including the Internet and phone.

Put a 'do not disturb' sign on the door.

Make sure you have access to drinks and snacks.

Light a candle, say an invocation to the muse, put on your special writing hat or create any kind of ritual to get you into the zone.

Writing is deep work. (Actually, there's a great book called *Deep Work* by Cal Newport, which you might find helpful.)

The more you can focus on your writing, the easier it will be.

WRITE ABOUT YOUR WRITING CAVE.

WRITE ABOUT THE TYPE OF RITUALS THAT HELP YOU FOCUS ON CREATIVE WRITING.

Decide that you will write in different places at various times until it feels comfortable to write wherever you are.

Chapter Nineteen

FOCUSED FREEWRITING METHOD

> "But anyone who has experienced flow knows that the deep enjoyment it provides requires an equal degree of disciplined concentration."
>
> —*Mihaly Csikszentmihalyi*

FREEWRITING METHOD FOR NOVELISTS

Writing your first draft should be done as quickly as possible.

The state of mind you need to be in is one of creative flow.

This means you don't edit, and you don't think.

Allow the words to flow out of you.

To write a first draft as fast as possible, you need to freewrite, using your outline as a springboard.

For thousands of years, the storytellers of a tribe spoke their stories aloud.

Often they had memorised them, but every story had to start out somewhere.

It had to have a moment of origin.

When I was at school, I often made up stories to amuse my friends.

To do this, I would start out with a rough idea of what I was going to say: a story hook, a character, a conflict.

A ghost wanted a girl to find his lost treasure, but her father has forbidden her to go into a locked room, or a naughty little brother flooded the house and then pretended his older sister did it—that kind of thing.

Then I would just let the words come out.

The secret to writing fast is to sink into a type of disciplined concentration and let it happen.

This is called freewriting.

Freewriting is a tumbling river of words.

You allow them to pour out of you.

But how?

As adults, we are in the habit of choosing our words carefully.

We learn to hold back.

As a writer, you have to relearn how to open the gates and let it all come out.

SKETCH THE SCENE FIRST.

Choose which scene you want to write.

You can write your novel in any order you like.

Many writers like to start at the end, getting down the final scenes first and then perhaps the main action scenes.

There are no rules.

Experiment.

Find out what ignites your creative fire.

When you've picked the scene you intend to write, have a look at how you've described it on your outline.

Next, make a sketch of the scene by listing it in a bit more detail.

Include setting, mood and an emotional turn.

Example: Looking at my outline of *Trappist 5*, I've decided to write the all-is-lost moment first.

The basic description is this: Paradox is on a virtual island inside the server.

She sees faces in the tidal wave as it bears down on her—the face of her grandson calling out for her and the face of the Koenig, mocking her for her recklessness and stupidity.

Remember, we said that recklessness was the shadow or negative side of her trait of Courage.

Using these basic notes, I make a list of the scene structure:

- Darkness. There is a single light on the virtual island. Paradox is on a tiny island, no bigger than her cabin. Sand under feet.
- The tidal wave looms in the distance.
- Show her fear. Flashback to when her lover drowned.
- She knows if she drowns in the virtual world, her heart will stop, and she'll die in reality.
- Lights in the wave form faces.
- The Koenig's face mocks her. Her fear escalates. She is certain she will die.
- Her grandson calls to her.
- Her fear turns to anger.

Include a brief note about the setting.

Notice how Paradox opens the scene alone and afraid.

Yet she ends it in a state of anger.

This is called the emotional turn.

Every scene should have one, even if it's very slight.

In this scene, I want my reader to believe that Paradox is in a hopeless situation.

And I leave it like that.

I don't wrap up with her overcoming the greatest obstacle in her story journey.

She is helpless and out of control. This is how your MC should feel at this point in the story.

Spend a couple of minutes imagining the scene as if you were watching a movie.

Make the pictures in your mind as clear as you can.

Turn down distractions.

Double-check that you won't be disturbed.

Set a timer.

A good length of time to freewrite is about 40 minutes.

Start with 15 minutes, or less, and see how it goes.

Then extend your freewriting time.

After a while, you might be able to write non-stop for an hour.

Once again, experiment.

This is your writing process.

There is no right or wrong, only your own creativity.

Find out what works for you.

Don't edit.

Write.

Don't stop.

Just write.

Don't edit.

Don't stop. You can clear everything up later.

Keep writing, and you'll surprise yourself with what comes out.

Don't worry about grammar, spelling or punctuation.

Open the gates of your creative mind.

Let the words spill out of you.

Enter the 'fictional dream' of the story.

WRITE. WRITE AS IF THERE IS NOTHING ELSE IN THE WORLD.

And if you can, practise speaking your story aloud using voice recognition software such as Dragon Naturally Speaking.

Dictating your book is the fastest way to write.

WRITING PRACTISE. SELECT A SCENE FROM YOUR OUTLINE. IT MIGHT BE THE OPENING SCENE, OR THE ALL-IS-LOST MOMENT OR ANY OTHER EVENT YOU WANT TO WRITE. CREATE A QUICK SKETCH OF THE SCENE. THESE NOTES WILL ACT AS YOUR WRITING PROMPTS.

Eliminate all distractions.

Even if you only have half an hour or less, sit down to write. Set a timer.

Imagine you are observing the scene unfolding, as if you are watching a movie.

Set your inner writer free and go write.

Chapter Twenty

WRITING FAST

"You know what, your imagination works faster than your mind."

—*Simona Panova*

Writing Fast

It's important to write your first draft as fast as you can.

Finish it one go.

It doesn't matter if it takes you a week, a month, a year or more, but do it as fast as time and life allow.

Having a story outline helps you do this, as does a routine of timed freewriting sprints.

Training yourself to write anywhere, anytime helps to develop a professional approach to your writing.

At first, sitting down to write 80,000–100,000 words might seem daunting.

Even if you plan to make a novella, you'll still have to produce 40,000–49,000 words.

Which is still a heck of a lot of wordage.

BE FEARLESS.

You can do this, and it will be fun, although not in the way that lounging around by a pool in hot weather is fun.

There is something incredibly satisfying about pushing yourself beyond any previous limits.

My first novel took me a few months to write, but I had no outline, and it didn't work as a story.

Several half finished manuscripts were abandoned after that.

Then I spent six years writing and rewriting the same book.

The reason it took so long was because I kept stopping and starting it. When I came back to it, I added a new plot point or revised the entire plot and started again.

Then I changed the character arc. After that, I introduced more characters, changed the setting and rewrote the outline.

On and on it went.

Everything I did was a learning experience, but at the time it felt like I was stuck in a horrible time warp, doomed to keep writing the same story over and over until the end of time.

Then I scrapped the idea of outlining and wrote my next novel in six months.

This book took a further three months to edit while I worked a proper story outline with a professional editor.

Finally, I had produced the best book I could write and published it myself. That was my writing journey.

You can save a whole lot of time and heartache by using a basic novel writing blueprint like this:

- Create an outline.
- Freewrite your first draft from this outline.

- Work with a professional editor to smooth out the story.
- Rewrite if you have to.
- Publish.
- Create an outline for your next book, refining your process as you go.
- Keep on calibrating as you create new stories.

The best thing about writing your first draft as fast as you can is that you keep a powerful connection with your original story.

I realise now that stopping and rewriting during the first draft phase is a common mistake made by new writers, which is related to self-doubt.

Banish all doubt.

Keep the faith.

Keep writing.

You can work out any problems later.

But you can never edit something you haven't finished.

THE MORE YOU WRITE, THE FASTER YOU'LL GET.

Even if you've already written a few novels, you'll always be improving your writing process.

There will come a time when you can be certain to finish a book in a set amount of time.

Many writers take a novel writing challenge every year in November.

It's called NaNoWriMo—National Novel Writing Month.

It started in the States but is available every year to anyone with Internet access.

The challenge is to write a novel of 50 thousand words in a month.

You'll get plenty of encouragement, hints, tips and support if you join this community.

It's a wonderful experience and free to sign up, so why not give it a go? Their website is a cornucopia of great stuff, so check it out at www.nanowrimo.org.

Visit the site anyway. NANOWRIMO has a lot of great information for writers. Make notes:

Keeping a Record of Your Word Count

I use Scrivener software to write my novels.

It takes a bit of time to learn how to use but is an amazing toolkit for authors.

The price is low and therefore within most people's reach.

When I first got hold of it, I found it confusing and couldn't see what all the fuss was about.

However, in the end, after hearing so many other indie writers talking about it, I made the effort to get to grips with it.

It's literally the best thing I did for my own writing process.

Have a look at it and see if it might be something you could use.

Scrivener has a function that allows you to track your word count as you go along.

You can set up goals for each writing session, with a deadline to work towards.

I find this helps me to stay focused on my work in progress.

If you don't fancy using Scrivener, you can always keep a word count in your notebook or a document on your computer.

I find it helps me a lot to know exactly how much I've written each day and how much closer each freewriting session gets me to the completion of a project.

Some writers don't like to work with word counts.

They analyse their progress in other ways.

Once again, experiment.

This is your novel writing blueprint, and you change it to fit your own creative needs.

KEEP A RECORD OF YOUR WORD COUNT FOR A WEEK. DOES THIS INSPIRE YOU TO WRITE? IF SO, KEEP DOING IT. IF NOT, DON'T: INCLUDE THESE HEADINGS: DATE/ TIME/ WORD COUNT/ DAILY TOTAL

Dictation

A lot of writers nowadays are using dictation to write their first drafts.

You can speak much faster than you can write, but it does take practise.

I use Dragon Dictate, but I'm still getting used to it.

I've written a couple of books with this software and found I could manage 8,000–12,000 words a day. It's quite expensive, and not everyone can work with it.

There is a period of 'training your dragon', where there will be a lot of misspelled words and strange interpretations of your input.

However, it's a great way to get through a draft, so I thought it was worth mentioning.

Remember this: Speed is the key to getting your first draft finished.

The quality of your work will be just as good.

Editing will sort out any issues.

Analyse your word count.

Note down the time you started and finished each freewrite session.

It also helps if you make a note of how you felt while you wrote. Many writers are surprised to find that their emotional state doesn't affect their writing.

You'll write just as well when you're tired as when you're not.

Try writing for short sprints.

Start with just 8 minutes.

Perhaps you write more words if you have shorter sessions with quick breaks in between.

NOW DO A LONGER SESSION. START WITH 50 MINUTES. HOW MANY WORDS DID YOU WRITE?

If you're a binge writer, cramming your writing time into weekends or holidays only, allow yourself some time to warm up and cool down.

You will write a lot more if you know you'll start slow, speed up and then wind down.

Chapter Twenty-One

WRITING SMART

"...on the job there was nothing but the job. You left the shit outside the door. You could always pick it up on your way back out."

—*Laurell K Hamilton*

Writing smart is all about focus.

Your mind is constantly in motion.

Paying attention to one thing for a long period of time is just a way of utilising that movement.

I know it sounds like a paradox - and that's because it is.

Focus is a disciplined kind of action.

With practise, you will be able to write for longish periods of time with the directed concentration of the sun through a magnifying glass.

Be careful, you might set fire to the paper.

TAKE A MOMENT TO WRITE DOWN ALL THE STUFF GOING THROUGH YOUR MIND RIGHT NOW:

We all have busy minds!

Be sensible.

Take breaks, go for walks and eat healthy food.

Taking time away from directed freewriting sprints is as important as doing the writing.

Don't forget to read.

Reading feeds your creative mind better than anything else.

We write stories because we love to read them.

You'll learn something about the writing craft every time you read a book written by another author.

Knowing when the MC reaches the first threshold increased my love of reading.

I enjoy seeing how other writers find ways to make each story beat different and fresh.

Focused freewriting is your magic spell.

All your preparation bears fruit as you write through your first draft.

Every time you sit down to write, you enter the world of your story.

The more curious you are about the sights, sounds, smells, tastes and feelings your characters might be having, the easier the writing will be.

Allow yourself to be fully immersed in the story you're writing.

There is a kind of magic in this phase of your novel writing process.

You are, after all, conjuring something from nothing, creating a new thing in the world. Elizabeth Gilbert talks about this in her book on creativity called *Big Magic*.

While you write, you are surfing the wave of your own imagination.

It's a great feeling.

A little strange at times, but that's how it should be. You are using your brain on full power, so relax, it knows what to do.

Take dictation from your unconscious mind.

ANALYSING YOUR WRITING PROCESS

Getting stuck happens to all writers at least once.

A block can be overcome by various different approaches.

Use writing prompts.

Each time you break down a scene into the initial sketch, you are making a list of writing prompts.

This means you can kick-start your writing by using more unusual prompts.

Surprise yourself.

Imagine a scene in your book where lightning strikes a tree, a woman falls in love with someone online, a man walks into a police station and so on.

Use writing to get you writing.

Write in your journal, on your phone or on a napkin.

After you've loosened up a bit with your writing, go back to your outline.

Is it working?

Could you strengthen the characters?

Make plot changes?

But don't spend too much time analysing at this point.

Finish it first.

Focussed writing is a form of creative meditation.

I agree with Natalie Goldberg's concept that writing is a form of meditation.

Anything you practise with flowing awareness is meditation.

Whether it's making art, running a marathon, building a house, baking a cake or writing a novel, when you freewrite, you are in an altered state of consciousness.

Personally, I like being in the zone.

For many years, I've practised meditation.

I've tried a few different types, experimenting and exploring.

Writers are, by nature, curious people.

We like to see things from lots of different perspectives. This is what you are doing when you write from the point of view of one of your characters.

In effect, when you're writing a novel, you put on someone else's shoes and walk in their feet.

To do this well, you have to get out of your own way.

When you're in the middle of a freewriting session, it feels like flying, and you know you're in contact with a deeper part of yourself.

There is some evidence to suggest that when your brain shows a predominance of calming alpha brainwaves, you are at your most creative.

These are the same brainwave patterns produced by meditators.

Alpha states are similar to daydreaming.

Freewriting is the open road to alpha states.

However you feel when you start, just keep writing. Don't think about what you've just written. Write the next word and the one after that.

As you do this, you become aware of everything.

All your gates are open.

You judge nothing.

If that's not mediation I don't know what is.

NB: TIME TO READ

What are you reading right now?

Read anything and everything.

Don't stick to one genre.

Read books about writing, art, travel, science, history and anything else that interests you.

After you've finished your next freewriting session, get a coffee and sit down for a relaxing read.

Enjoy reading like a writer.

What can you use?

What ideas do you have while reading?

I'm not talking about plagiarism. You can learn so much from other writers as you absorb their work.

WHAT ARE YOU READING RIGHT NOW? ARE YOU ENJOYING IT? WHY? WHAT CAN YOU LEARN FROM THE AUTHOR?

When your first draft is finished, you can begin editing.

Some writing books suggest putting your manuscript aside for a few days or longer before you start editing.

It's a different part of the process, and it might work for you to mark this transition by taking a break from your story.

MAKE NOTES ON HOW YOU WILL APPROACH THE EDITING STAGE OF THIS BOOK:

As always, experiment. Find out what works for you.

Try different ways even if you think you know what works best. I like to begin the edit right away, while the story is still really fresh in my mind, but I used not to.

Celebrate finishing a first draft. It's an amazing achievement.

Congratulations.

Part Four

EDITING

Chapter Twenty-Two

EDITING SWEEP 1: STORY

> "When you write a book, you spend day after day scanning and identifying the trees. When you're done, you have to step back and look at the forest."
>
> —*Stephen King*

Editing doesn't have to hurt.

You just need to develop a healthy relationship with it.

Do it a few times and with the right intention and you'll begin to enjoy it as much as any other part of the creative process.

This is the time of reaping, of refinement, of completion.

HOW DO YOU FEEL ABOUT EDITING? IF YOU DON'T MUCH LIKE IT, HOW CAN YOU ENJOY IT MORE?

Editing Sweeps

After years of editing the novels of new writers, I've streamlined my own technique.

The next few chapters will explain this technique. Try it out for yourself.

You might want to change it and refine it so it fits your own needs as a writer.

However, I strongly suggest you do a variation on the concept of separate editing 'sweeps'.

A sweep is when you're looking at one aspect of your book.

Print it out.

I like to start editing as soon as I've finished the first draft.

That way, the story is still fresh in my mind and in my dreams.

Many writers like to put the manuscript away for a while, to get away from it and come back when it's risen, like putting bread dough in the airing cupboard.

Try both methods and discover what works for you.

Then do this: Print out a copy of your book.

Feel the weight of it in your hand.

You've made a new thing in the world.

Print out a copy of your outline as well.

EDITING TASK 1: SWEEP 1: STORY

Read through your story from the perspective of how well the story works.

Some scenes might work better in a different order.

Make notes in the margin of your manuscript about anything related to story structure.

Ask yourself the following questions:

DOES YOUR FIRST ACT LAUNCH THE BOOK? DOES IT INTRODUCE THE MAJOR CHARACTERS, INCLUDE A TRIGGER EVENT AND SHOW THE READER THE PRESENCE OF THE ANTAGONIST?

AT THRESHOLD 1, HOW HAVE YOU SHOWN YOUR MC MAKING A DECISION? IS IT FOLLOWED BY SOME KIND OF JOURNEY?

IN ACT 2, HAVE YOU SHOWN YOUR MC'S WEAKNESS? HAVE YOU SHOWN HIM PLANNING, HIDING, RESPONDING, TRAINING, RECRUITING, OBSERVING AND ANALYSING?

AT THRESHOLD 2, WHAT NEW INFORMATION DOES YOU MC DISCOVER? WHAT DOES IT MEAN TO THEM? HOW DO THEY TURN TO FIGHT THE ANTAGONIST IN ACT 3?

HOW HAS ACT 3 BROUGHT YOUR MC TO HIS KNEES? WHAT IS HIS ALL-IS-LOST EVENT? CAN YOU MAKE IT WORSE? IF SO, HOW? WHO IS HER ALLY AT THE END OF ACT 3?

WHAT CHOICES IS MC FACED WITH AT THRESHOLD 3? DOES HE MAKE THE RIGHT ONE FOR THE STORY YOU ARE TELLING? IS THERE A THRESHOLD GUARDIAN OF SOME KIND?

WHAT SACRIFICE DOES YOUR MC MAKE IN ACT 4? DOES IT SEEM BELIEVABLE? WHAT IS YOUR LAST LINE? DOES IT BRING YOUR STORY FULL CIRCLE?

Go back to the electronic version of your story. Make any changes you need to.

Chapter Twenty-Three

EDITING SWEEP 2: CHARACTER

"Like a cruiseship slowly turning, the story will start to alter course via those thousands of incremental adjustments."

—George Sanders

Every sweep adds strength to your manuscript.

I'm sure you can see that each time you go through your story, you'll notice and change something.

With a good outline, your story will be robust, and as you made the changes in Sweep 1, you improved your book.

This is not the time to get caught up in grammar and punctuation.

You are still taking a more global view of your work. As you tighten it up, you begin to see the polished version emerge.

Characters bring your story alive. Your MC reacts to problems, fails, fights, plans, fails again and sacrifices some part of herself to compete the story cycle.

Now it's time to look at how you've shown the thoughts, words and actions of the characters in your story.

Editing Task 2

Sweep 2: Character

Read your manuscript through again. This time, answer these questions:

HOW HAVE YOU INTRODUCED YOUR CHARACTERS IN TERMS OF THEIR STORY ROLE/ARC?

HAS YOUR MC SHOWN HER POSITIVE CHARACTER TRAIT?

DOES SHE HAVE A DISTINCT VOICE OF HER OWN?

DOES THE ANTAGONIST?

WHAT ABOUT THE MINOR CHARACTERS?

IS THERE A ROMANTIC SUB-PLOT? IN A ROMANCE, IS THERE A MYSTERY, PARANORMAL, HISTORY-BASED, FANTASY OR SCIENCE FICTION SUB-PLOT?

CHECK DIALOGUE. EVERY CHARACTER SHOULD SPEAK IN HIS OR HER OWN PARTICULAR VOICE. IN A GAME OF THRONES, THE AUTHOR DOES THIS REALLY WELL. ALL OF HIS CHARACTERS SOUND DIFFERENT. MAKE NOTES ON YOUR MANUSCRIPT AS YOU READ THROUGH.

CHECK CHARACTER ARCS. DOES YOUR MC CHANGE AT THE END OF THE STORY? HE MIGHT NOT NEED TO, ESPECIALLY IF YOU'RE WRITING A THRILLER OR DETECTIVE SERIES.

HOW DOES YOUR MC ACT IN DIFFERENT SITUATIONS? DOES SHE SHOW HER WEAKNESS? COULD SHE BE MORE ACTIVE? LESS?

HOW DOES YOUR ANTAGONIST ACT IN DIFFERENT SITUATIONS? DOES HE SHOW HIS GOOD SIDE?

After you've made improvements to the characters in your main manuscript, you're ready for one last edition sweep.

The work is almost done.

Chapter Twenty-Four

EDITING SWEEP 3: LANGUAGE AND STYLE

> "If it sounds like writing, I rewrite it. Or, if proper usage gets in the way, it may have to go. I can't allow what we learned in English composition to disrupt the sound and rhythm of the narrative."
>
> —*Elmore Leonard*

This is when you look at the writing itself. During this last sweep, you need to look out for things such as sentence structure, spelling conventions, grammar, punctuation and style.

Sentence Structure

In action scenes, make good use of short, punchy sentences.

Vary the length of your sentences.

Watch out for typos.

These can be much harder to spot than you think, and some of them have a way of eluding all but the most hawk-eyed of proofreaders.

If you self-publish, you can always bring out later additions to correct these.

However, pick up as many of them as you find. You want this book to be good quality on every level.

If you can afford it, arrange for a proofreader to look over your work when you've finished your last sweep.

This is also the time to think about working with a professional editor. In my experience, editors are like midwives. They want your story to come out alive and healthy.

Spelling Conventions and Word Usage: British-English vs. American-English Spelling

The easiest way to deal with this is to write in your version of English.

Sometimes I use American spellings, but mostly I spell words such as *colour*, *centre* and *flavour* the way I always have.

Word usage is a different thing.

If your story is set in Britain, and you are an American writer, make sure you are tuned into what things are called over here.

The same goes for British writers setting a book in the States, Australia, or other English speaking countries. Train your eyes and ears every time you read a book or watch a film or TV series.

Consider what words a particular region use for specific things.

Editing Task 3

Read through your manuscript one last time.

This time you must READ IT ALOUD. Some writers record themselves reading each chapter to make the most of this editing sweep.

Reading a story aloud is the best way I know of finding errors in language and style.

HAVE YOU READ YOUR STORY ALOUD AND MADE ADJUSTMENTS ACCORDINGLY. MAKE NOTES.

That's it. Your story is made.

It's almost finished, but not quite.

A few final touches are necessary. It is ready to send to an editor.

Chapter Twenty-Five

OUTSOURCING TO AN EDITOR

> "Editing is a kind of creative activity where, in a perfect world, an author and an editor find that elusive oneness to understand each other intuitively."
>
> —*Sahara Sanders*

Outsourcing to a Professional Editor/Line Editor/Proofreader

This is a big step in the writing process.

There are a few different kinds of editors you might like to work with, depending on what you can afford and the type of edit you need. For example, you can get a structural edit, a copy edit, a line edit or a proofread.

Structural Edit

A structural edit is the same as your editing sweep 1 and 2 combined. This is an expensive option but well worth the money if it's one of your early books. Remember, your writing will improve with every book you write.

Don't be too proud to ask for help, especially at the start of your novel writing adventure.

Sometimes it feels as though the story isn't working, but you don't know why or how to fix it.

A structural editor will check your story outline as well as the manuscript.

Expect the editor to send you a detailed report on characters, story beats and theme. The editor will offer suggestions for changes to help you fix any issues around character and plot.

DO YOU NEED A STRUCTURAL EDIT? IF SO, MAKE A LIST OF POSSIBLE EDITORS:

Copy Edits and Line Edits

An editor who offers this service will investigate every line of your story in terms of language and style.

This is a thorough examination of the writing and definitely worth the investment if you can afford it. Expect to receive a marked up, electronic copy of your manuscript. Some editors will correct grammatical and punctuation errors as well.

MAKE A LIST OF COPY AND LINE EDITORS:

Proofread

Even when you've tweaked your book to the best of your ability, hire a proofreader.

They should be able to mop up the last of those pesky typos.

MAKE A LIST OF PROOFREADERS:

When you get a report back from an editor, it's time for the final piece of the process.

You must tweak your book one last time..

Part Five

REWRITING & PUBLISHING

Chapter Twenty-Six

REWRITING

> "When asked about rewriting, Ernest Hemingway said that he rewrote the ending to A Farewell to Arms thirty-nine times before he was satisfied. Vladimir Nabokov wrote that spontaneous eloquence seemed like a miracle and that he rewrote every word he ever published, and often several times. And Mark Strand, former poet laureate, says that each of his poems sometimes goes through forty to fifty drafts before it is finished."
>
> —*Susan M. Tibergien*

Rewriting

This is your chance to make the last changes to your book.

If your editor has suggested some rewriting, and you agree with her suggestions, then make the changes.

I like working with editors, despite the pain they sometimes inflict. The first novel I wrote with a serious view to publishing needed a complete rewrite. I had not written a proper outline, so the story didn't work.

Rewriting is the same as freewriting.

Take the new outline and settle into the zone.

With luck, you might only have to rewrite a few scenes to improve your story. That's great. If you have to make a lot of corrections to the grammar and punctuation, you'll absorb ways to write it better next time.

Nothing is wasted in the rewriting of your novel.

You might even enjoy it.

I did, although it was tough at times.

New Ideas and What to Do about Them

If you have any new ideas during your final analysis of your editor's report, check them out with your editor first.

WRITE DOWN ANY NEW STORY IDEAS YOU HAVE AT THIS POINT:

Read aloud.

After you‘ve made your final corrections, read your finished manuscript aloud, if possible.

When you’ve done this, your book is ready to meet its readers.

You might want to send it to a few friends, family or other writers who have agreed to read it for you.

Beta Readers

Beta readers will look over your work from the point of view of the reader.

Readers are special.

They are the reason you've written your book, particularly if you want to publish.

Cherish any feedback you get from anyone kind enough to read your book before it comes out. Ask them if they could leave a review on Amazon when it comes out.

Working with a Cover Designer

If you have experience in graphic design, you might like to make your own covers.

If you are hoping to publish with a traditional publisher, the publisher will design a cover with its in-house specialist.

RESEARCH COVER DESIGNERS AND MAKE A NOTE OF THEIR DETAILS:

However, if you're planning on publishing your book yourself, I strongly advise you to pay a professional to do your cover for you.

There are some reasonably priced cover artists online, for example, at fiverr or 99designs.

As a writer, it's fun to work with other creatives.

I always enjoy this experience. Be courteous as you experiment with different designs and artists. Research other covers in your genre. Remember, it's best to fit in as well as to stand out.

Make sure the cover makes an impact, as well as conforming in some way to the reader's expectation of the genre.

At every stage of your novel writing blueprint, you are aware it can always be calibrated.

A blueprint that sees you through to the end of making your book into a reality is one to be treasured.

Use it each time you want to write a novel, and you'll achieve your goal.

Chapter Twenty-Seven

PUBLISHING YOUR NOVEL

"Once, if you told people you were self-published, they'd look at you like you were a smelly old jobless hobo just come off a dusty boxcar with soupcan shoes and a hat made from a coyote skull."

—*Chuck Wendig*

SELF-PUBLISH AND BE BLESSED

Even if you are smelly hobo with a coyote skull hat, this won't stop you from publishing a professional novel and making enough money to buy real shoes and a blanket.

This book is primarily about the craft of writing, so I won't say much about this side of things.

However, when your book is finished, you need to decide what you want to do about publishing it.

Personally, I think anyone who writes, edits and self-publishes a novel with a good cover deserves a basket of fruit, jewels or kisses.

Self-publishing is a long game.

You play it by consistently writing the best books you can.

It might be a novel every two years, or it might be two books a year. You might get up steam and write more than that.

For most new authors, it takes time to create books. But after a while, you'll get a following of dedicated readers, which means that when you publish your next one, people are waiting to buy it.

If you self-publish, you maintain complete control over your copyrights.

This means you can update the work, change cover designs and do anything you like with it. A lot of indie authors write in a series, which is popular with readers.

You are responsible for the entire creative production of your book when self-publishing, which is both exhilarating and hard work. As I said, it's a long, interesting, exciting, creative, life-changing kind of game.

In 2017, self-published ebooks outsold the traditional publishers for the first time.

This seems to show a trend towards e-readers on a global scale. The same thing happened in film a few years ago when almost all of it became digital. Nowadays we download movies rather than going to the video store.

More and more readers are getting access to the global market in books.

Through Amazon, Kobo, iBooks and others, your work can be enjoyed by people from the far north of the world to the far south and back around. These are wonderful times to be an author.

Formatting and Uploading

If you choose to self-publish, you'll have to format and upload your manuscript and book cover to a site such as Amazon or Kobo. A lot of authors use Draft2Digital instead because they do the formatting for you.

I format most of my books myself, but I'm a control freak.

You can read more about the self-publishing and marketing side on Joanna Penn's brilliant website at thecreativepenn.com. Mark Dawson helps a lot of writers with the marketing side and advertising platforms.

You can listen to his podcast and Joanna Penn's on iTunes or watch them on YouTube. There is a brilliant atmosphere of camaraderie in the indie community. Writers are helping other writers all the time.

After you've formatted and uploaded your book, it should be available for sale within a day or two.

Traditional Publishing

There are many good reasons to go the traditional publishing route.

You might want to see your novel in major bookstores around the country, raise your profile and possibly be put forward for a literary prize.

Perhaps you like the idea of not getting involved with cover design choices, editing and marketing. In-house editors come free. It's a lot less work.

Some bestselling indie authors also publish a few of their books through traditional publishers.

For those of you who want to get published by a traditional publisher, this part of the process is much slower than indie publishing. Instead of two days, it will take around two years for your book to go on sale.

Your royalty share is also much lower.

This means you have to sell a lot more books to make a reasonable return on your creative time and energy.

Your book will be on sale for a limited time in paperback format, and then it will be withdrawn.

Nevertheless, if this is the path you want to take, do the research.

Most publishing houses won't look at unsolicited manuscripts.

This means you'll need an agent first. If you have a few self-published books that are selling well, all the better.

LAST THOUGHTS

Whichever way you go when it comes to publishing, remember to start writing your next book as soon as you can.

The greatest reward is in the journey from idea to finished book. In the creative fire of prewriting, freewriting, editing and in making something new in the world—I believe—you'll find true happiness.

Becoming an author takes time and energy.

There is always something more to learn when it comes to story creation.

Every writer knows that they can keep on improving until the final curtain falls, so make a commitment to keep studying the craft and the art of writing.

It's an intense, exhilarating journey. And every story you create is better than the last, so go create . . .

NOTES ON MY PUBLISHING JOURNEY WITH THIS BOOK. WHAT WENT WELL? HOW COULD I IMPROVE NEXT TIME?:

AFTERWORD

Notes at the End of the Book

Jill taught Creative Writing at the Open University, developed and taught various novel writing courses and is developing an online novel writing course to go with this book.

She has also been an avid reader all her life.

Like most writers she's always made notes. Her house is full of diaries, journals, notebooks and scrawls on bits of paper everywhere.

After a few years of teaching creative writing, she decided to put everything she'd been teaching into practice.

This led to a career writing and publishing her own novels and non-fiction books full time.

She has learned to love every stage of the process, however difficult it might appear to be at first.

Most of all, she's come to the conclusion that the secret to writing books is this:

- Make your mistakes out loud. Don't be afraid to make changes to a published work in order to make it better. Know that you are always improving at your craft.
- Enjoy discovering your own writing process. To that end, make sure you experiment with all kinds of outlining techniques, freewriting sprints and methods of rewriting.
- Find an editor you feel really comfortable with. However, even if you like your editor; if she or he doesn't do a good job for the price you paid, move on.
- Above all, make the books you love to read for the readers you love.

You can find me, and get your free book - 10 Books Every Author Should Read, on my author website at www.narrativebeats.com.

A warm thank you to all my readers, both fiction and non-fiction.

If you have time, I'd really appreciate it if you could leave a review on the site where you bought this book.

Made in the USA
Lexington, KY
21 July 2019